LIVE. LEARN. GROW.

Life's in Session!

Turn up the volume on your life.

By

Robin H-C

Be weird. Be random. Be who you are.

Because you never know who will love the person you hide.

Author Unknown

www.lifesinsession.ca

Disclaimer

This book is not intended as a substitute for the medical advice of a physician. The reader should regularly consult a physician in matters relating to his/her health and particularly with respect to any symptoms that may require diagnosis or medical attention, both physically, and emotionally.

This book is not intended as therapy and though the author believes in the opinions of this book, if you are under psychiatric care or in therapy it is strongly advised that you consult your therapist or psychiatrist for agreement prior to incorporating any of the suggestions within the chapters.

Any advice taken from this book is applied with free will with the understanding it is the readers choice to experiment with the tools, philosophies and opinions in this book after consulting with a medical expert.

Publisher: Humans Winning at Life /Oct. 2013 2nd Print Run

Distribution: books@lifesinsession.ca

Editorial: Matt Rott   Jacket Photo: Jason Stead

Cover layout/design: Andrea Markusich / 99 Design

Speaking Engagements/Author Comments:

Robin@humanswinningatlife.com

ISBN 978-0-9733646-6-8

Life's in Session!

You are here to learn lessons. The world and people in your life are your teachers. Just like in high school, some teachers and lessons will be welcome and very compelling. Others may have you question the entire education system!

The most valuable lessons you receive will initially be very difficult to embrace. Embrace them anyway, for they are the biggest gifts in your life and the access to greater self awareness that contain the seed for a powerful life breakthrough. Try as you may, you cannot hide from these lessons.

I don't know for certain that things happen for a reason. What I do know, is that when you invent a reason it can give you tremendous power over a situation. When you take on the philosophy, *'it's meant to be'*, it eliminates resistance and suffering and has you search for reasons that can propel you forward in this exciting adventure called Life.

There are two key emotions that drive us in life. Fear and love. Fear is the underlying source with emotions such as anger, worry, frustration, apathy, jealousy, addiction and depression. Love is the key operating principle–emotion presents within courage, kindness, trust, generosity, risk and positive change.

In order to shift from fear to love possibility must be restored. To restore possibility in any area of life one must release past experiences and beliefs to become open to see and feel what is truly possible in this area. Know this: what you focus on will expand.

We are all subject to unwelcome experiences. At the end of the day, you are either a person who looks for ways to turn things around or a person who justifies why life's not fair – if you are the latter – it is never too late to switch teams!

Never consider the possibility of failure; as long
as you persist, you will be successful.

Brian Tracy

Thank you

Joni, I like you & I love you. I choose you & I chose you.
Heaps of love & gratitude to a remarkable Mother.

Andrea Markusich, Schwess; My greatest cheerleader, for your
partnership, listening & crazy humor.

My Zen Monkey, James, you continue to teach me so much
above love & kindness.

Malcolm & Sue-Mom, forever enthusiastic & proud.
We are absolutely thrilled you are moving to Toronto!

Lisa & Jeremy Taggart, for your unwavering loyalty &
friendship.

Warren Porter, you entered my life in 2001 and have not left
my side since.

Robert Gignac, author of Rich is a State of Mind, for your
tireless generosity, leadership & edits.

To my clients, past, present and future: You honor me by allowing me the privilege to work with *You, your Teams* and to be your partner in success and transformation.

To Jack Canfield, Wayne Dyer, Deepak Chopra: for the plethora of inspirational resources you have gifted the world that inspire myself (and many others) to be more, to give more, to learn more and ultimately, to love more. Thank you.

And finally, to my readers: Thank you for purchasing Life's in Session. Please allow this book to become a resource for guidance in your life. Hold it in your hands, think of something you would like to better understand, and allow a number to come to mind, or simply flip open to a page. You'll notice your unconscious has directed you to a soothing quote or a life principle, that is rather fitting for your current situation.

Gratitude bestows reverence, allowing us to encounter everyday epiphanies, those transcendent moments of awe that change forever how we experience life and the world.

John Milton

Chapters

Better Living Assignments...1

Beliefs & Unlearning...15

Career & Money Practices...................................29

Environment 39

Go With Life...49

Health & Nutrition...61

The Invisible World...73

Love in Action...85

Logic & Reason...99

Mind Body Spirit...113

Mysteries & Interesting Facts...........................127

People Power...139

Powerful Practices & Habits...............................151

Raising Little Adults......................................163

Rejuvenation & Play.......................................177

Relationships...189

Stop it!..203

Tools, Distinctions, & Resources..........................215

Time Management...229

Zen Wisdom..239

Life's in Session!

You can teach a student a lesson for a day; but if you can teach him to learn by creating curiosity, he will continue the learning process as long as he lives.

Clay P. Bedford

Better Living Assignments

It is in the moment of action that change exists.

Give Compliments Freely

Today – wherever you are, whomever you're with – give a compliment. "My, that suit is stunning," or "your face lights up when you talk about your passions." A compliment is not to be confused with obsequiousness – I'm talking truly, authentically beginning to notice the positive and simply sharing what you've seen. This action has the power to bring people out of a funk and add levity to your day too. Notice something wonderful, something you truly appreciate in another, and say it out loud.

A compliment is verbal sunshine.

Robert Orben

The Inchworm Theory

Life is a heck of a thing to happen to a person! It often seems like the eternal list of things to do is constantly being added to, and it is and will continue to be incomplete. Truth be told, you'll have days when you experience uncertainty and dissatisfaction – days when you are overwhelmed. So where do you start when you have a thousand ideas or tasks to manage? Simple: You begin with a pen and a stack of cue cards. Write one task or idea per cue card, place them in priority sequence and address one card at a time. Not certain which idea or task you should take on first? Choose each card randomly until you've finished the pile. It's the Inchworm Theory and it gets you there every time.

The man who removes a mountain begins by carrying away small stones.

William Faulkner

Life Begins at the End of your Comfort Zone

Cross your arms...yes, right now, cross them. Once you've done that, cross them the opposite way. How does it feel? You'll find that one way feels natural while the other is completely foreign. After folding them the alternate way several thousand times, that too will eventually feel comfortable and become normal. What's this got to do with your life? Resistance to change is very much governed by your comfort zone. Just because something is comfortable does not for a moment mean it's what you want, or even good for you for that matter. Many are comfortable being in debt, overweight or cranky. So how is this information helpful? What if you were to begin associating change with discomfort? That's right – every time you forego the chocolate cake or make that cold call for business you could begin to correlate and embrace the pain of discomfort with actively applying the success principles. You could consciously create a neural association between discomfort as proof that you are carving a new path, because Life's in Session!

Life begins at the end of your comfort zone.

Neale Donald Walsch

Evaluate Your Decision Making Process

All of our actions are driven by one of the following: the desire to feel better, to honor a comfort zone, or to eliminate anxiety. A trip to the gym is designed to get that workout high or the feeling of being in control of your toned body. People reach for cheesecake for the wonderful sensory experience. Of course, that glass of merlot may help ease your worries momentarily. Many shop to cheer themselves up. Today, more than ever, we're a quick fix society drawn to immediate gratification. It's important to check in with your decision making process. Is it working for you? If you're having that dessert and you're already dissatisfied with your weight, it is likely that sensory enjoyment will turn into guilt within a few moments of swallowing the last morsel. Shopping while knowing you are running up debt creates anxiety no matter how much you love your new golf clubs or designer purse. Take charge of your life by controlling your choice-by-choice behavior. Create a power statement. Repeat to yourself some version of this: "I feel a sense of self-mastery and pride when I choose to be health, wealth, or choice conscious."

Do not bite at the bait of pleasure till you know there is no hook beneath it.

Thomas Jefferson

Impulses, Urges, & Cravings

Begin to bring awareness to the cravings and urges you're subject to daily. By not acting on impulses you further develop control and self-mastery. It may be giving up a coffee, bypassing a fast food restaurant, or perhaps ignoring a mood you may be tempted to engage. There's tremendous power in declining an emotional pull, and this is especially true with energy depleting habits. When you practice resisting an urge you exercise the ultimate in self-control until everything eventually becomes an option. What are you really craving? Fulfillment, love attention? Restore your power by challenging yourself to say "no" to the things you normally don't resist – until things that once were not become a conscious choice.

As I grow older, I pay less attention to what men say.
I just watch what they do.

Dale Carengie

Your Point of View is Decisive

Grab your notebook and make a list of things you view as a major life problem – things you struggle with that interfere with an outcome you desire. Now jot down an explanation for each problem. Explain why you view it as an issue, what has you feeling defeated about it, or how it is ruining your life. Now, rewrite the problem, only this time identify the opportunity within it. Could it be this is exactly what you need to expand an underdeveloped part of yourself? Is there a lesson it's inviting you to learn? The truth is, the problem is not actually the problem – it's the view point you've taken in regard to the problem that is causing you stress. This is most likely some version of: "It's impossible...I'll never...It won't work...It shouldn't be...I tried before..." Shift your point of view and the problem is then available to be morphed into an exciting challenge and an opportunity to showcase your transformational skills.

Opportunity is missed by most people because it is dressed in overalls and looks like work.

Thomas Edison

Limit Your Vent Time

You're only human – it's okay to vent your frustrations and acknowledge your disenchantment. It's also a sign of positive emotional fitness to release things. It's important to become conscious of how much time you spend complaining. At one time or another we've all met an Energy Vampire – that is, someone who nags or complains constantly, draining the life from even the most inspiring of conversations. Frankly, they can be bothersome to listen to and exhausting to be around – be it you or someone else. The things we do repeatedly easily become habit, and this includes complaining. When you frequent a mood your body and brain becomes conditioned to a chemical frequency. Eventually this chemical process becomes a part of your biochemistry. In a nutshell, your body learns to expect it. Make it a rule to spend no more than 5–10 minutes venting in a conversation (when necessary), and then move on to brainstorming on ideas and solutions, embracing whatever situation is challenging you to grow.

The point is to change one's life. The point is not to give some vent to the emotions that have been destroying one; the point is so to act that one can master them now.

Barbara Deming

The Wake Up Happy Ritual

Cheerfulness is absolutely a learned behavior – as is pessimism. Plan your morning such that you train yourself for positive expectancy throughout the day. This may involve listening to "*you can do it*" music or inspiring audio CDs en route to work. Attend an early morning spin class. Recite your affirmations or re-visit your mission statement. Begin a daily ritual that supports mindfulness and positive life anticipation. A few positive intentions in the morning have the power to influence the entire day.

Won't you come into the garden? I would like my roses to see you.

Richard Brinsley Sheridan

Why Wait?

Steven Levine said, "If you had one hour to live and one phone call you could make, who would you call? What would you say? And what the heck are you waiting for?" We operate as though we have an eternity to set things right with people. Stubbornness and fear may never subside, and you can act in spite of them. Today, apologize to someone or acknowledge what they have brought to your life, for they may not be around when you finally find the perfect words, time, or courage to do so.

Forgiveness does not change the past, but it does enlarge the future.

Paul Boese

Response - Able

When you experience someone in your environment that is angry or frustrated, the natural response is to mirror their emotion and then blame them for setting the tone. In other words, Re - ACT. So next time your partner, your boss, or even a stranger challenges you with an unfavorable mood, do your best to observe them without judgment. It is possible to witness the behavior and be unaffected, and sometimes even contribute to the shift of another person's mood. Begin by simply recognizing the emotional state of another without making them wrong or expecting them to be any other way than exactly how they are at that moment. Internally connect with compassion and step back, removing yourself from their physical space. It may not always feel like it, and it does take practice, but you do have a choice of how you respond to people and the moods they present.

If a small thing has the power to make you angry,
does that not indicate something about your size?

Sydney J. Harris

Be the Hero in Your Own Life

Are you waiting passively for something to happen before your life gets better? Do you secretly hope that someone is going to rescue you? Are you praying for a financial windfall that'll wipe away your eternal worry? Are you one of those who attract people who become your projects, cleverly distracting yourself from your own core issues? Or maybe you're awaiting the perfect partner that will keep you smiling and dancing merrily on your plateau of heavenly bliss forever and ever, amen. Kindly excuse the giant pin that is about to burst your bubble! What you seek it is not outside of you. The most valuable treasures are cultivated from within, not without. The fruits of these treasures manifest externally only when you begin to connect with your timeless essence and nurture yourself above all else. It begins by learning to make yourself happy and becoming accountable for all that you *do* and *do not* have in your life right now. How can YOU become the Hero in your own life? Today, identify one action that can help you come through for the most important person in your life – YOU!

We do not have to become heroes overnight. Just a step at a time, meeting each thing that comes up...discovering we have the strength to stare it down.

Eleanor Roosevelt

Agonize or Adventure

Have you ever agonized over a decision? You were so consumed with making the right choice that paralysis set in and you neglected to make any choice at all. Humans are binary and function best with two choices. Anything more can trigger a state of being overwhelmed, and for some even two options are too many! Now, it's perfectly natural to be unsure when making a major life change. A career change, moving to a new country, or choosing to get married – these are all significant decisions that will have a profound effect on your life and your future. But here's what you need to remember – there is no right choice. Every experience is your very own personal adventure. Right, wrong, good, and bad are all interpretation. There is never a guarantee that any choice will work out as planned. And guess what? If necessary, you can make a correction and amend your decision in the future by making another choice. Learning happens through experience. Forget about making the right choice and simply make a choice.

Don't take life too seriously. Nobody gets out alive anyway!

Toni Watson

A Daily Gratitude List

Gratitude is an emotional expression of an appreciation for all that you have. It's the process of focusing on *what's there*, not *what's missing*. Periodically, take a few minutes to prepare a list of everything you're grateful for. Some days your list will be easy, with so many obvious treasures to acknowledge. Unequivocally, there will be also times when you feel you have very few things to be grateful for. It's on days when you are not tuned into gratitude that your riches can become most apparent. Most of us take for granted blessings such as vision, a relatively healthy body, food in the refrigerator, and friends to lend an ear. Turn on the news for five minutes and you will be quickly reminded that although your life is far from perfect, you always have much to be thankful for.

We can only be said to be alive in those moments when our hearts are conscious of our treasures.

Thornton Wilder

Beliefs & Unlearning

We are so trained in the thought system of fear and attack that we get to the point where natural thinking -- love -- feels unnatural and unnatural thinking - fear - feels natural. It takes real discipline and training to unlearn the thought system of fear.

Marianne Willaimson

Immediate Gratification

So much is instantaneous in today's world. You can decide you'd like a summer home in the Hampton's at 9:00 AM and by the end of the day you've been pre-approved for a second mortgage. Fed up with learning to lose weight? Book the appointment for liposuction and pay for it on your credit card. For those of you who are tired of aging, you can have injections to hide that it's happening…and so our society goes. There are bank commercials that induce excitement: "You are richer than you think!" Sure – if you're willing to remortgage and subsequently spend your house! We have lost our long-term focus and are addicted to the quick fix, feel good highs available in the 21st century. There's a reason it takes nine months to have a baby. The time in between is a preparatory stage. Now, I'm not implying that one should give up all immediate gratification, but it is possible to take the perspective that things that take time are developing some wonderful surprises and strength of character. Consider: it is not just the outcome, but who you become in the process of accomplishment. Let's keep a bit of balance in this day of fast food and instant credit, people!

Adopt the pace of nature, her secret is patience.

Ralph Waldo Emerson.

The Joy Transition

Some people literally have to be taught positive expression. Joy, playfulness, and pride – among other positive emotes – are modeled for us by the elders in our environment (provided you were fortunate, that is). If you grew up with a parent prone to depression or mood swings, being joyful is likely not a natural way of being for you. The emotions modeled to a young child generally become the easiest to express throughout life. Was your environment adept at expressing anger, fear, anxiety, or worry? Pay attention to what you are comfortable expressing – it's probable that you're reliving the dominant emotions of your childhood unconsciously. If you're truly interested in transforming these patterns, it may be time for an interference strategy. Check out the movie *What the Bleep Do We Know* as a place to begin to deeply understand your emotional frequencies, humanness, and the brain-body biochemistry.

The most useful piece of learning for the uses of life, is to unlearn what is untrue.

Antisthenes

Understanding Beliefs

Beliefs are created when information is stored in the brain during heightened emotional episodes. If the unconscious mind accepts a piece of information fed from the conscious mind, this results in a belief – something we believe to be true. It becomes a self-fulfilling prophecy. For example: "Losing weight is hard." In reality, losing weight is not hard, yet this is a widely held belief. "Hard" is an interpretation. For some, looking in the mirror at a heavy person or eating toxic food that slows the metabolism is hard – more so than making healthy choices that result in a lean physical disposition. "Resisting junk food is hard" may be a more accurate communication, or even "finding motivation to exercise"; still, they are beliefs all the same. Throughout life you'll become associated with such beliefs through memories stored in the brain's archival system. These can define who you *think* you are and influence your actions, causing an outcome to appear or disappear. Beliefs are undone the same way they are created. Begin to examine what you're saying internally that interferes with your results and immediately begin transforming those conversations.

It's the repetition of affirmations that leads to belief. And once that belief becomes a deep conviction, things begin to happen.
Muhammad Ali

Reconcile the Goal

Richard, a sports broadcaster, said he wanted a life partner – to be in love – yet at the same time he wanted to be free to see people when he was on the road, which was six months of the year. Cindy, a mother of three, said she wanted to be a children's author, writing about values such as self-esteem and courage – yet she lived a life of fear and isolation, secretly using drugs on a daily basis. Kim swore she was committed to her healthy lifestyle and complained of her struggle to lose weight. In public she would eat salads and exercise, but at night she would go home and binge on Ding Dongs and ridiculous amounts of ice cream and candy, thereby making weight loss impossible. Check to see if you have an ulterior motive that may be interfering with what you'd like to do, be, or have. Is there a belief in the way that is serving as a road block? If so, are you ready to do the heavy lifting necessary to remove it? In most cases, it's unlikely you can be both, or you would have done so by now. You must give up one in favor of the other.

Self sabotage is when we say we want something and then go about making sure it doesn't happen.

Alyce P. Cornyn-Selby

Conditioned Beliefs

Do you realize that if I say, "Politician" or "Money" you have a series of neural association that are instantly triggered? You may believe politicians are creepy, or you may see them as leaders who deserve more credit. Perhaps Bill Clinton comes to mind as one of our best orators, or you may have strong opinions about his personal life. This is information storage – a complex process your brain has set up to interpret the world. What about money? Is money easy to make? Hard to come by? Maybe it doesn't grow on trees. Think for a moment. What's the source of that information? Do you agree with the information you've been repeating to yourself? The point is, whatever you feel about these two topics is based on information activated from a retrieval system from your conditioned memory. It stores information and opinions input from a variety of sources, and has been doing so since infancy, true or not. In fact, without your conscious permission your brain has designed these highly intricate archives that are being accessed every few seconds in order to evaluate and assess what things mean in your environment.

> *For me, it is far better to grasp the Universe as it really is than to persist in delusion, however satisfying and reassuring.*

> *Carl Sagan*

Did you know there's an emotional state and physical posture that accompanies each thought pattern you have? For example, when you put your pajamas you probably enter a state of relaxation. When wearing business attire you may shift into a more methodical disposition and notice your productivity levels multiply. You may even choose different language. Sweat pants may follow with an urge to exercise, or they could signify the need to mentally decompress. Each one of us has a series of brain patterns that induce an emotional state. Try having a lazy day at home in your business attire and chances are you'll be in work mode, grappling with the urge to take care of business. Think about it: What if you were to attend a job interview in your bath robe? How much enthusiasm and confidence do you think you'd exude? So put this into your long-term memory treasure chest for when you may not feel 100%. The simple task of grooming – be it particular clothing, shaving, makeup, or hairstyles – can induce a positive mental state and have you feel better instantaneously!

The self-image is the key to human personality and human behavior. Change the self-image and you change the personality and the behavior.

Maxwell Maltz

Mantra

A few years ago I took a well earned break from a busy travel schedule to flee to Nassau, Bahamas. I had a delightful trip. During my travels absolutely everything seemed to go my way. One after another, things fell into place. On my last afternoon, after shopping in town, I stopped in for a delicious frozen beverage at my hotel. It was then I met Jack, the owner of the helicopter tour company in town. Jack insisted on flying me to the airport so I could see Nassau from a helicopter before leaving, something he said everyone must experience. The trip had gone so well for me, and for a split second I recall thinking, "What if something goes wrong?" It was then I realized that I was uncomfortable when too many things went my way. Thus, I would almost expect something to go wrong, and in due course was more likely to attract it. After identifying my thinking pattern I came up with a replacement mental slogan – "What else can go right?" It only took a few moments to test it out: When I arrived at the airport for check in, I was bumped up to business class!

I never came upon any of my discoveries through the process of rational thinking.

Albert Einstein

Agreement Verses Possibility

Reality is determined by agreement, but agreement does not automatically mean truth. In 1954, Roger Bannister achieved what was considered impossible when he ran a mile in under four minutes. The moment he did this he changed what was possible in people's minds. Since that time, many athletes have followed suit. Today it is said that becoming pregnant at the age of forty or older is statistically unlikely. Yet people do it. I suspect a few decades from now it will be increasingly common based on the evolutionary norm. If you want something, don't give the past the power to dictate what is possible for your future. Create the conditions to make it happen.

The saddest aspect of life right now is that science gathers
knowledge faster than society gathers wisdom.

Isaac Asimov

Learned Limitations

Imagine that at birth a baby elephant is tied up to a tree with a chain that gives it about a 30-foot radius to wander before it encounters resistance. After a while, that chain can be replaced with a thin rope that the elephant could easily break, yet the elephant, having learned its perimeter, stays within the radius of the original chain. Placing a flea in a jar offers a similar example. After several attempts to escape, a flea will quickly learn of the jar's ceiling and teach itself to jump just below it. When the lid is removed, the flea will remain in the jar, not recognizing that it could easily jump higher to freedom. An invisible limitation – information learned in one situation that no longer applies or exists in reality is brought to life through belief and memory. In this context, people are no different from the elephant and the flea examples. Metaphorically, is there a chain or lid governing your experience because you've trained yourself to believe it still exists?

If you truly want to understand something, try to change it.

Kurt Lewin

Trauma and Letting go

Cassy was a vibrant young lady with a passion for fashion. By twelve years old she had made several outfits for herself and her friends. She openly shared her vision to move to New York City and become a world renown designer. Sadly, at 14, Cassy was raped. The rapist told her "she was too pretty and was asking for it." After this, Cassy put away her sewing machine and began to dress in boys' clothing – she would not longer groom herself. At 18 she refused to attend her prom. When it came time to register for college she instead opted to train to become a security guard. Worried, her parents insisted she seek support. During group therapy, another patient asked her how long the abuse had lasted "Ten minutes" she replied. "Ten minutes, and you've punished yourself for five years. You've become a different person, you won't date, you dropped your passions, and you've basically built your identity around one horrible incident. What he did was awful, but what you're doing to yourself is outright cruel." Cassy began to sob. Moments later she broke into laughter, the beginning of the end of tragic experience that had haunted her.

What we give our attention to stays with us. What we let go of, will let go of us.

Cat Forsley

Guidance

Contrary to popular belief, it is not necessary to accomplish an outcome in order to guide or coach someone else to success. Think of the professor that teaches European history who's yet to spend significant time in Europe. Oprah Winfrey had not mastered weight loss, yet she successfully inspired millions to lose weight, slim down, and tone up. Doctors and health practitioners routinely initiate healing practices in their patients, never having struggled with the illness themselves. What about a professional football coach who instructs his players to do things he has never been, nor ever will be, capable of physically performing? There are many results you can help others to achieve, even if you have never personally triumphed in an identical situation.

It's a terrible thing to see but have no vision.

Helen Keller

Preacher Perfect

Do you know someone who thinks they're perfect? They point out every time you have something that contains sugar or preservatives, which they'd never consume. They ride their bike everywhere to save on emissions and take advantage of every opportunity to educate you on recycling, diet, nutrition, and the latest environment faux pas. Aspiring to become more aware of one's self and the planet is indeed an admirable path, but pushing it on other people can come across as imposing and self-righteous. Even the most commendable message goes unheard when delivered through an arrogant medium. Let's give people the space to learn what it is they need to learn as they're ready, and always be generous with whatever stage people are at – even the bossy ones!

If a man should happen to reach perfection in this world,
he would have to die immediately to enjoy himself.

Josh Billings

View Point

A little boy was heard talking to himself as he strolled through his backyard, wearing a baseball cap and carrying a ball and bat. "I'm the greatest baseball player in the world," he said with enthusiasm. Then he tossed the ball up in the air, swung, and missed. Undaunted, he picked up the ball, threw it into the air, and said to himself, "I am the greatest ball player ever!" He swung at the ball again, and once again he missed. He paused a moment to examine the ball and bat carefully. Determined, he once again threw the ball into the air and said, "I'm the greatest baseball player who ever lived." He swung the bat as hard as he could and again missed the ball. "Wow!" he exclaimed. "Unbelievable! What a great pitcher!"

Author Unknown

You can discover more about a person in an hour of play than in a year of conversation.

Plato

Career & Money Practices

Normal is getting dressed in clothes that you buy for work and driving through traffic in a car that you are still paying for - in order to get to the job you need to pay for the clothes and the car, and the house you leave vacant all day so you can afford to live in it.

Ellen Goodman

Financial Vision

By tuning into the benefits of achieving your financial targets, you'll naturally intensify your motivation and activate choices consistent with achieving the outcome. Look at it this way: Would you give up your impulsive shopping habit in favor of a rustic lakeside cottage...? I thought so. Keep in mind that you'll become more inclined to budget as you develop a clear vision of what it means to your life over the long term. Make a list of all the compelling reasons to meet your financial goals and check in weekly to acknowledge the action based choices (ABC) that bring you one step closer. You can begin a visual support by creating a collage or folder with pictures of your dream property, both inside and out. Don't forget to tell the tale of lifestyle and location, and be sure to get specific. Now, bring this all together in the form of a plan that you can watch actualize as you follow it – day-by-day, step-by-step.

The breaks you need in life wait within your imagination. Imagination is the workshop of your mind, capable of turning mind energy into accomplishment and wealth.

Unknown

Money Sense & Creativity

If you're worried by the financial implications of Christmas or birthdays, get resourceful! The last thing you want is a financial hangover arriving with your January Visa statement that can linger for months to come. There are many ways to make memorable gifts with the investment of time, creativity, and love. Honor your budget and activate your creative side by designing a music CD of favorite songs or a video montage of your best life moments with someone you love. Frame a photo of a fond memory and include an inspiring quote. Make a list of the "Top 100 Things I Love About You!" or playful personalized coupons for, well, you name it! Well thought out homemade gifts are among the most cherished. People soon forget a tie or socks, but will remember forever the letter you wrote with an open heart.

Frugality is one of the most beautiful and joyful words in the English language, and yet one that we are culturally cut off from understanding and enjoying. The consumption of society has made us feel that happiness lies in having things and has failed to teach us the happiness of not having things.

Elise Boulding

The Game of Giving

Regardless of how much wealth you have accumulated to date, consider that every time you're financially savvy you can easily generate funds to be endowed to others. Be it $10.00, $100.00, or $100,000.00, this is now money you can direct to make a difference for people and causes in the world. Why not give it a go? Pick a cause you're passionate about and play the giving game. You can do it with time or money. Get others involved and create a community event. After all, the best thing you can do for people in need is to not be one of them – then you can play the giving game and offer a helping hand.

I don't think you ever stop giving. I really don't. I think it's an on-going process. And it's not just about being able to write a check. It's being able to touch somebody's life.

Oprah Winfrey

Frugal Fun & Cheap Thrills

Begin a list of inexpensive, playful activities that spice up your life. You might cash in your air miles for something you may not normally purchase. Begin a "movie share" program with your neighbors. Go to the local Aesthetics College for a massage or a manicure offered at a quarter of the price. You could return your refundable bottles and treat yourself to a second-hand book or a savory non-fat Green Tea Frappuccino at Starbucks. Instead of a dinner out, how about a picnic at the park or a weekly potluck in your community? There are a plethora of unexplored creative options to have fun while you save and develop a greater sense of wealth consciousness. What are they for you?

Wealth is the ability to fully experience life.

Henry David Thoreau

Wealth Management

Managing money and respecting the money you have is an affirmation of wealth. Some of the wealthiest people I know are the people who clip coupons. They only dine out on two-for-one entree night. They look for bargains and wait for things to go on sale, and only then do they make their purchase. They check the bill to make sure it's accurate, and if it's off by $2.00 they'll say something and have it corrected. They pay attention to every cent and, though they could, they don't throw money around like a big shot.

It's no coincidence that 90% of the world's wealth is held by 10% of the people.

Bob Proctor

Get Personal

As you are aware the business world is filled with human beings. As such, being a great leader in business involves the ability to develop and understand the people in your environment and to connect with them on many levels. The simple practice of remembering people's names and personal details about their lives goes a long way, and this is not limited to the people you have direct contact with. If your client mentions his daughter Sydney's graduation, jot that down and inquire at your next meeting. Get to know your colleagues and clients outside of their position. Be personable. Look at it this way: If you have an opportunity to do business with someone you like versus someone you are not fond of—and in all other regards the product being offered is the same—chances are you are going to give the business to the person you like. It's simple: Be likeable.

The deepest craving of human nature is the need to be appreciated.

William James

Tools for Teams

A fundamental principle in motivating teams and individuals to peak performance begins with acknowledging the full spectrum of human being. Simply stated, your career impacts your home life and your home life in turn impacts your career. It is unavoidable. Understanding this inevitability − and nurturing individuals as a complete evolving entity − supports optimal achievement in one's business activities while providing remarkable resources applicable to other life environments. If you're a manger or leader who wants their team to thrive, provide them with tools for life.

When you choose to be pleasant and positive in the way you treat others, you have also chose, in most cases, how you are going to be treated.

Zig Ziglar

Great Ideas

Next time you're driving, look out the window and notice a few things within eyesight that were once un-manifested ideas. Imagine how much effort went into believing or convincing investors of the possibility of a car, a light bulb, the Internet, or even the windshield wiper. Before anything can become a household item it is first a crazy idea that some brave soul had courage enough to purse. Believe it or not, having a great idea is the easy part. Without brilliant action and fortitude, great ideas generally amount to nothing. Do you have a great idea? Then focus on cultivating determination and momentum, and above all else get the information to the right people who can support you in executing the idea and bringing it to the world. You may believe in your product 100%, but you will need to match that belief in yourself. Very few entrepreneurs get lucky, but the successful ones get busy!

Take up one idea. Make that one idea your life – think of it, dream of it, live an idea. Let the brain, muscles, nerves, every part of your body, be full of that idea, and just leave every other idea alone. This is the way to success.

Swami Vivekananda

Going the Extra Mile

This is a business practice that is guaranteed to set you apart from your competitors. Most people are out for what they can get, not what they can give. They deliver what they promise, and no more. What if you were to throw in a little extra during every business interaction? I call this going the extra mile. Now, what you can offer will vary depending on your business. If you are a real estate agent, obviously you are not going to throw in an extra house—but you can offer a bonus of three months of lawn maintenance or a fabulous gift card. Perhaps you present a quote for $100,000.00 for your software, and when your client receives the invoice he is delighted to notice a $5000.00 new client discount. If your business is service oriented, you might offer a coupon for a complimentary service for the next visit. As a landlord you may include a gift basket or flowers to each new tenant. Each of these gestures makes YOU feel good and serves to reinforce that it was a good idea to do business with you.

You can start right where you stand and apply the habit of going the extra mile by rendering more service and better service than you are now being paid for.

Napoleon Hill

Environment

The real key is to live in an environment where the mind feels free to choose the right thing instead of being compelled by habit and inertia to choose the wrong thing.

Deepak Chopra

Feng Shui

Feng Shui is the strategic placement of objects to best allow energy to flow throughout an environment. It's also credited with balancing out the natural elements such as fire, wood, earth, and water in one's space to attract additional wealth, joy, love, and so on. Once exclusive to the elite in China, it's now common for large corporations around the world to consult a Feng Shui specialist while designing their offices. Today, regular folk may also have an expert as part of their design team when creating an environment conducive to the specific function of the space. Give it a Google or pick up a few books at your local bookstore and see how strategic placements in your environment can shift energy flow to expand what's possible in your life.

We begin to see, therefore, the importance of selecting our environment with the greatest of care, because environment is the mental feeding ground out of which the food that goes into our minds is extracted.

Napoleon Hill

Reading Energies

I've had the opportunity to speak to thousands of people in many locations around the world. As such, I have learned to feel and read energies. While speaking in hospitals, I developed an awareness of the energy variation from say a hotel conference room where people often gather to celebrate. Hospitals and prisons, for example, tend to carry a collective darkness. That's no surprise, given they are both inhabited by large groups of people with their attention on the morass of life. Entering different spaces, I can feel the heaviness, a sinister foreboding force – much like entering a room where someone has just received horrible news, the residual impact of thought energy. When house shopping, you'll likely notice the varying "feelings" depending on the moods or lifestyles of the occupants. A house on the market for an expanding brood may feel different than one that's on the market due to divorce. It can still look appealing, but it may be missing that...*je ne sais quoi.* Get acquainted with the energies that people and spaces carry. Learn to read these invisible frequencies and connect only with those that work for you.

We should not pretend to understand the world only by the
intellect: we apprehend it just as much by feeling.

Carl Jung

41

Clean House

Imagine if you were to set aside an hour to rummage through your closets, basement, and garage this evening. How many things do you think you could discover that are currently not in use and haven't been for some time? Unused items generate stagnant energy, can deplete inspiration, and can be draining to look at. The average person can find a few thousand dollars worth of re-usable items in their home. How wonderful it is to de-clutter your space and turn your bygones and baubles into cash. So dust off your precious collectables, have a garage sale this weekend, post a few items on e-Bay, or simply take a trip to the Salvation Army or the local shelter. I promise you'll feel better for it! As a result of cleaning house, you can pay a bill early or splurge on something you may otherwise not indulge in – a fancy lunch, a new golf driver – or you could even sponsor a child overseas (www.children.org) or send a few dollars to the Make It Right foundation (www.makeitrightnola.org). The key is to make every penny count – even if you have billions, trillions, and quadrillions of them!

How wonderful it is that nobody need wait a single moment before starting to improve the world.

Anne Frank

Productivity Trick

Here's a tip for being more productive, especially when you work from home. Choose an area to work from and make a rule that whenever you sit down in that spot you only do work. No Internet surfing, no social calls – you are programming your mind to be unconscious by allowing only one activity to reign in that location. If you find you've engaged more frequently in distractive behavior – for whatever reason – change locations. This is an NLP practice of training yourself to associate a particular space with a predictable outcome.

If you do not conquer yourself, you will be conquered by self.

Napoleon Hill

Make Room for a Happy Future

Emotionally charged objects can set a tone for your life. Leslie lived in a house she had shared for years with her husband. After they split, she took on sole ownership of the property. One day while we were in session I noticed her staring at a painting – her thoughts looked painful. "What does the painting remind you of?" I asked. She replied with tears, "My husband and I bought that on our honeymoon. Now, it reminds me he is with someone else – someone half my age." We then had a talk about emotionally charged items, and the unconscious pull they have over us. A week later when I returned for our Coaching appointment, the painting had been removed and placed in storage, along with several other "reminders." Leslie appeared vibrant and alive. I inquired what had shifted. She told me she recognized that as beautiful as the painting is, it currently represented the breakdown of her marriage. She went on to say that although at some time in the future she may appreciate it for the beautiful art that it is, today she could not. Leslie realized that moving forward would be easier without passing painful emotional triggers several times per day.

Let's not forget that the little emotions are the great captains
of our lives and we obey them without realizing it.

Vincent Van Gogh

44

Group Energy

Have you ever been to a stadium for an event when the team is on a winning streak? Perhaps you had the great fortune to visit the London 2012 Olympics, or an NBA or NHL game. It really doesn't matter what sport, or whether you've played it or even like it, for that matter. The energy created when people come together to collectively focus on a common goal is fantastically undeniable. The magical force from this invisible field can be felt instantly upon entering the venue. So go to an event and cheer for something – anything. Ignite your enthusiasm while connecting with the best of humanity, cheering for life, for love, for each other to win.

I love to hear a choir. I love the humanity…to see the faces of real people devoting themselves to a piece of music. I like the teamwork. It makes me feel optimistic about the human race when I see them cooperating like that.

Paul McCartney

Pets and Energy

According to Feng Shui principles, pets absorb energy. Of course, this makes sense – it explains why we often see pet owners and their animals with a similar temperament. The aggressive biker with the pit bull that charges everything or that sweet little old lady with a docile poodle that won't stop licking you. How about the dog that is jumping on you, completely out of control? An obvious reflection of the owner's life. Animals mimic and absorb human characteristics and emotion. An ancient Chinese practice is the cathartic use of goldfish in one's environment. Fish help by cleansing and absorbing negative energies. Odd numbers of fish are said to be ideal in this specific practice. If you have a cat or a dog – really any pet you are fond of – you may want to bring some fish into the equation, particularly when going through stressful periods in your life. Allow the fish to absorb some of the stagnant yang energy of the household. If (or when) they pass, it is customary to celebrate with gratitude the energy they absorbed for you.

Be it human or animal, touch is a life-giving thing. Has anyone ever had a stroke or a heart attack while cozied up with a pet? I doubt it.

Robert Brault

Caring for Your Planet

We can all do our part to contribute to greater planetary awareness. Reuse those papers with writing on one side because you recognize it's a tree. Walk or ride your bicycle a bit more, as doing so limits the production of airborne toxins and restores the ozone. Take that one can out of the garbage because you understand that although it's only one can, if five million people a month say the same thing, annually that's 60 million cans a year that end up in landfills, which could cover the state of Texas. (I just made that up but I'm sure it's a lot!) Do your part to respect our planet for us, and for future generations.

*I would feel more optimistic about a bright future for man if he spent less time
proving that he can outwit Nature and more time tasting
her sweetness and respecting her seniority.*

Elwyn Brooks

Energies & Balance

We've all engaged disparaging thought energies at one time or another. Here's what you can do about it when you are stuck in an undesirable mental maze: Open the window in your office, car, or home. Energies have powers beyond what we recognize, and it's likely to clear faster with fresh air flowing through. Think about it: If you sit in a chair that someone else has just occupied, it is warm. This warmth is caused by body heat – lingering energy. Make no mistake: The invisible has tremendous power, and energy does loiter, which is fine if it's positive. But it is important to cleanse the alternate the moment you become aware of it. Salt is said to neutralize stagnant energies, so consider a bath with sea salt or place a small bowl by your desk or area of reoccurring stressors. Try listening to spa music, doing some baking, or pick up a fresh cut floral arrangement. A few drops of vanilla in boiling water smells like freshly baked cookies. Purchase a sage smudging stick – to cleanse negative energies from the environment. Discover what works best for you. Basically anything that changes your mood can clear or alter the energetic balance of a room.

No matter where you go or what you do, you live your entire life within the confines of your head.

Terry Josephson

Go with Life

Happiness can exist only in acceptance.

George Orwell

Choose What Is

Life is really about choosing what is while creating what you want. Resisting anything is a guaranteed formula for suffering. As you accept all situations life throws at you – just as they are – peace becomes an option. So your house burnt down and life feels unfair – it is, but choose it anyway. Your father is critical and nags constantly – choose him. He's not likely to change, but you can. Resisting reality is a surefire recipe for pain. Choosing "what is" is the only way to end suffering. When you choose life, people, and events exactly how they are (and how they are not), an opening becomes available for power to be restored. Today, direct your valuable life energy into building that which you can control – which is always YOU – and your response to that which inevitably, simply IS.

The strongest principle of growth lies in the human choice.

George Eliot

There Are no Do-Overs

How many of you are waiting for your real life to begin? I was supposed to be an actor, a millionaire by 35, married, an entrepreneur, a parent, retired by now, skinny! If only I had parents that had celebrated my successes instead of my failures, life would've been so much easier! If only – if only. Sound familiar? We all have some version of *if only,* but ruminating on the "what ifs" of yesteryears*?* One word: redundant. Okay, four words: redundant and life sucking! Though we've all wished for it at one time or another, there are no do-overs in life. You are where you are, you have what you have, and the sooner you reconcile this reality, the better off you will be. In any area of life, whatever the obstacle, the only place you can begin is here – right now with your current life scenario exactly as it is. In fact, this is the perfect place to begin; the only place you can begin. So gather up your life lessons – yes, even the stubborn ones you'd prefer to resist – and live like today is the first day of the rest of your life.

Feeling sorry for yourself, and your present condition, is not only a waste of energy, but the worst habit you could possibly have.

Dale Carnegie

Funerals – A Reminder to Live

Dan attended a funeral for his good friend's sister Diane. She was 52, and by all accounts everyone had expected she'd have many more years ahead of her. Sadly, she did not. On the way back from the funeral, Dan found himself very pensive. He was contemplating life and death – specifically, how some people seem to die ahead of their time. "Do they know they are going to die? If they did, would they do things differently?" Dan reflected. Upon arriving home, he dusted off an old business plan on his desk. It had been sitting dormant for years. He'd always dreamed of starting his own business, but the fear of failing had overwhelmed his ability to take action. Dan became inspired to make the most of his life after Diane's funeral. By the end of the day he had a domain name, a website in progress, business cards ordered, and a list of potential clients to approach. He had also written his letter of resignation for his current job. Dan pondered: "Perhaps funerals are not just about saying goodbye. Perhaps they are also there to remind us to live as though we are going to die one day."

Those who danced were thought to be insane by those who could not hear the music.

Angela Monet

A Happier YOU!

People historically believe their joy and happiness depends on what happens in life. The truth is, it's never what happens to you, but rather how you respond to and what you choose to say to yourself about *what happens*. In reality, there is likely nothing that transpired in the past that can prevent you from empowering a positive mental attitude at this very moment. Understand that your happiness is ultimately determined by how you look at your current life conditions and what you opt to do, independent of unwelcome character building circumstances and personal history. Happiness has everything to do with our response – ability versus circumstance. Knowing this, is there a new inspired approach you can apply to an old experience that will result in a happier existence or an instant recourse?

Your living is determined not so much by what life brings to you as by the attitude you bring to life; not so much by what happens to you as by the way your mind looks at what happens.

Kahlil Gibran

Opportunity

Rachel was a stay at home mother of three who aspired to be a writer. During the Olympics she was compelled to write a letter acknowledging the athletes, their passion for their chosen sports, and their commitment to their countries. In the letter, she shared how she and millions of others were touched by being able to witness this level of achievement. The network she sent it to was encouraged by the letter and posted it in the Olympic Village. Soon after, she was contacted by a well known broadcaster and asked to discuss the letter on air. When I spoke to her she said, "I can't, it's too much, too soon." I responded, "So it's like this, Rachel. You put it out there that you want this, right? It's like you asked the universe for $10,000.00, and it responded – but instead it offered you a million dollars. It must expect you can handle the million". Rachel went on about how she was not ready and couldn't possibly do live radio, until I interrupted: "This actually isn't about you – it's about your message, remember?" When you put something out there and an opportunity finds you, trust there's a reason, get yourself out of the way, and ACT!

I think luck is the sense to recognize an opportunity and the ability to take advantage of it... the man who can smile at his breaks and grab his chances gets on in life.

Samuel Goldwyn

The Story of Kayga and the Zen Farmer

A Zen farmer and his neighbor Kayga were sharing a cup of green tea on a Tibetan mountaintop. Kayga noticed the farmer's prized workhorse running away. "Oh look, your workhorse is gone! How bad!" The farmer wisely replied, "It could be good, could be bad – we don't know yet." A few days later the farmer's workhorse returns, followed by 20 wild stallions. "Your horse brings you luck", said Kayga. "This is good." "Well Kayga, it could be good, could be bad." Soon after, the farmer's son was trampled in the field leaving the boy badly injured. "Oh no!" said Kayga. "Your son will take months to heal – such bad luck." The Zen farmer replied: "Could be good, could be bad – we don't know yet." A few days later, on a trip into town, Kayga noticed signs posted stating that all healthy boys were to be sent off to fight at war. "You're so lucky your son was injured," said Kayga. "After much consideration, I now see this is good." The Zen farmer looked over at Kayga, "Have you not been listening my dear friend? It could be good, it could be bad – we really don't know yet."

All meanings, we know, depend on the key of interpretation.

George Eliot

The Wake-Up Call

If you're suffering in any area of life, stop it! Find the courage to distinguish this as your wake-up call. Waking up after being numb or unconscious for any length of time can be difficult – painful, in fact – but what's more painful is continuing to live the same way once you've become aware, and silently observing yourself doing so. Suffering, similar to pain in the body, is an indication that things are out of balance – a call for change. Some people even suffer over how much they're suffering. How ridiculous! Be responsible for transforming this – knowing you can, and because deep down I'm certain you want to. Come clean with the people in your environment – tell one on yourself. Give yourself this taste of freedom and new people and opportunities will instantly show up. Your world will shift. Whatever your challenge, relate to it as "the past." Declare your new way of being aloud, and share your commitment to transition with the people in your life. Give yourself permission to get excited for the opportunities that exist. It's time to envision, strategize, and take action towards your ultimate life, one step at a time – no one else can do this for you.

People have a hard time letting of their suffering. Out of a fear of the unknown, they prefer suffering that is familiar.

Thich Nhat Hanh

Transforming Patterns

We all have patterns and ways of being that don't work. They may surface as being resigned in an area of life or shutting down when people get too close. An important awareness around any pattern is to understand that it won't leave while you're criticizing it – you cannot bully it away. A pattern needs appreciated and forgiven. Any current pattern in your life was born through a failure. You took a risk, failed to produce an outcome, then unconsciously created a way of being to deal with it. It's simply a survival mechanism that turned into a habit. When the brain and body memory senses a threat, it behaves in a way it believes to be protective, in order to cope – presto, there's your pattern. Bottom line – you will need to love any pattern before it can disappear. Pick a pattern or a way of being and identify how it was set up to protect you. Have a meaningful chat with the part of yourself that created the pattern. It may sound like this: "Thank you for wanting to keep me safe, I appreciate all you have done and I'm ready to let go." You'll be amazed at how quickly freedom can arrive after repeating this exercise while taking positive action.

Be kind to your shadow.

Rebecca Lawless

Dissatisfaction

Being dissatisfied is not entirely for not. When you identify the area of dissatisfaction, it can be a tremendous catalyst for change. It's like having a rock in your shoe: You can ignore the rock and expect a blister and pain along the way, and complain constantly about the rock, or you can remove it, thus creating a more comfortable journey. As a rule, dissatisfaction is a reminder that there is something you're doing (or not doing) that can make a difference to your peace of mind. The problem is that when you act powerless – like there is nothing you can do to change it – you in turn become powerless by means of how you think about it. Take a glimpse into where you may be discontent and what the message is telling you to act on, switch-up, or perhaps even let go of.

It isn't the mountains ahead that wear you out, it's the grain of sand in your shoe.

Unknown

Golf Analogy

Golf is a remarkable analogy for life. Known to be a frustrating sport at times, golf is a series of 80–150 swings over a four- to six-hour period. If you slice it the wrong way on the second hole and are still talking about it on the 10th, you are allowing the past to interfere with and determine the future. With each shot, one benefits from moving forward from the last one, bringing one's full attention to the current moment – focusing on the "now." Some people get stuck on a poor shot and allow it to influence the rest of their game. Others are experts at taking one shot at a time – they have fun, regardless of whether the last shot landed in the stream or the bunker. How's your game going? Do you remember to chuckle at a bad swing?

They throw their clubs backwards, and that's wrong. You should always throw a club ahead of you so that you don't have to walk any extra distance to get it.

Tommy Bolt

Life Lessons

There will be moments in life when you are presented with opportunities to grow past a part of yourself that no longer serves you. As illustrated in the movie *Groundhog Day* with Bill Murray, a similar person, experience, or event will show up over and over again until you accept your lesson and choose to address life from a new level of self.

It takes two to speak the truth – one to speak, and another to hear.

Henry David Thoreau

Health & Nutrition

Poor health is not caused by something you don't have; it's caused by disturbing something that you already have. Healthy is not something that you need to get, it's something you have already if you don't disturb it.

Dean Ornish

Food for Fuel

Some of us forget the purpose of food is to fuel the body. Each meal you have does not need to top the last one, nor does it need to give birth to your taste buds. Being picky about meals for some can be a symptom of general life dissatisfaction. Others refuse leftover's as if something that has spent a day in the fridge no longer offers nutritional value, or implies lack of wealth. What a luxury indeed to be born into a part of the world that offers an endless variety of fuel sources. Become mindful of what you put into your body knowing – it's a source of support for your brain chemistry, for your mood, and for your life.

The most remarkable thing about my mother is that for 30 years she served the family nothing but leftovers. The original meal has never been found.

Calvin Trillin

The Nutrition Lifestyle Challenge

Contrary to popular belief, improving your lifestyle does not need to be a painful experience. You can begin making changes to improve your health immediately in the smallest of ways. Make it a game to forgo the mayonnaise or cheese on a sandwich; eat only half of your French fries or have water instead of soda pop. You could begin enjoying an open-faced sandwich to cut back on empty carbohydrates. Today, with many people having a wheat allergy, lettuce is a refreshing alternative to wraps and buns – and it's GMO free. Challenge yourself in little ways to give up some part of your meal that's nutritionally void and look to increase the feel good foods that support your brain and body to thrive.

The doctor of the future will no longer treat the human frame with drugs,
but rather will cure and prevent disease with nutrition.

Thomas Edison

Stress Strategies

It's perfectly normal to experience periods of stress in your life. Here are a few valuable tips to support you during the process. Increase lean proteins – when under stress, the body automatically burns more protein, so be sure to up the amount in your diet. Remember to breathe deeply. One of the first things people tend to do when they are stressed is to shallow their breathing, limiting the amount of oxygen available to the cells. This stress response automatically compromises oxygen intake, which in turn lowers the immune system and fogs optimal thinking. Another important detail to remember: When the body undergoes its stress reaction, stomach enzymes slow in production. For those of you who are emotional eaters, it's important to be selective. If you must consume something, try a green veggie juice, pineapple, or some variation of a snack high in enzymes to aid digestion. Better yet, just get yourself to yoga class!

Pain is a relatively objective, physical phenomenon; suffering is our psychological resistance to what happens. Events may create physical pain, but they do not in themselves create suffering. Resistance creates suffering. Stress happens when your mind resists what is...The only problem in your life is your mind's resistance of life as it unfolds.

Dan Millan

Drive-Byes – A Weight-Loss Secret

Connie had struggled for years with her weight. She did exercise, but would hit a drive thru several times a week when she was exhausted and hungry. More often than not this was late in the evening. Her exercise efforts were neutralized by her late night consumption of nutritionally void, high calorie, fatty foods riddled with toxins too intricate for easy digestion – especially during periods of inactivity. In the spring, Connie was diagnosed with high cholesterol and heart disease. She was told to drop 30 pounds and consume a low fat, healthy diet – a blessing in disguise. The first change she knew she needed to make was fast foods. She replaced the term "drive thru" with "Drive-Byes" and instantly began to feel a sense of power and pride, and a connection to her growing vitality each time a she passed one. She would visualize a lean body, perfect skin, and self-control. Within three months she had met her target. She was amazed at how many people commented on the vibrancy she exuded. All from making one minor life change – the label, "Drive-Byes."

The truth is that we can learn to condition our minds, bodies, and emotions to link pain or pleasure to whatever we choose. By changing what we link pain and pleasure to, we will instantly change our behaviors.

Tony Robbins

Blood Type Diet

Much like stress, happiness is a chemical process in the body and there are choices you can make to best balance your own body chemistry. A book entitled *Eat Right for Your Blood Type* by Dr. Peter D'Adamo is a fantastic resource for foods indigenous to the geographical origin of your bloodline. His book offers a list of optimal, neutral, and interfering food choices tailored to specific blood types. Educate yourself on foods your body can most easily assimilate. Manage the dietary choices best aligned with your body type for optimal nutrition. The A bloodline, for example, descends from Asia. Thus, A types easily process fish, tofu, vegetables, fruit, and rice products, and fare well as vegetarians. Products such as steak and cheese are on the avoid list, as they tend to slow down the A type metabolism. The O bloodline, on the other hand, is the carnivore of the group and can process most meat efficiently. Try it out. This isn't to say you need to eliminate everything that's on your avoid list, but it is helpful to know what foods support easy weight loss and overall health. And of course limit interference foods, especially when dealing with external stressors.

Life expectancy would grow by leaps and bounds if green vegetables smelled like bacon.

Doug Larson

Salad is not Synonymous with Healthy

If you're taking on your nutrition, beware of the so-called salads at the deli counter. Though your intentions may be honorable, picking vegetables or salad does not automatically constitute a wise choice. Most deli salads are loaded with mayo, sugar, sodium, and preservatives – none of which amount to an easily digested, low fat, or nutritious meal. Several restaurants salads are equally misleading, containing up to 1300 calories and 40 grams of fat. Did you know many vegetable dishes today exceed the caloric content of a cheeseburger and French fries? Start the practice of reading labels. Never assume the contents of what appears to be a healthy dish without first checking the ingredients. And remember, the average salad dressing is filled with low grade oils and plenty of unhealthy fats, so be sure to order the dressing on the side and take control over unnecessary calories and GMO's. Healthy living becomes much easier when you are well informed and choice conscious.

The way he treats his body, you'd think he was renting.

Robert Brault

Fast Food

It's certainly not uncommon for people with busy lives to find themselves regularly consuming meals of compromised nutritional value. These days, every second business on a main street is a fast food location, making this type of fare the easiest choice – but at what cost? What you eat directly impacts how your brain and body function, which in turn will determine how you feel, how you look, and ultimately how you perform in life. Many of you will not notice the feel good impact available until you begin to limit or ideally eliminate such foods. To avoid the common fast food pitfall, all you need to do is prepare. Keep almonds, walnuts, or trail mix in your car, desk, or briefcase. Toss a banana or apple in your bag as you leave the house. Fast food does not need to compromise your health – it needs to be nutritious and convenient. By implementing this practice even half of the time, you will quickly experience a difference in your energy level and likely the ability to deal with stress more effectively.

We must pay greater attention to keeping our bodies and minds healthy and able to heal. Yet we are making it difficult for our defenses to work. We allow things to be sold that should not be called food. Many have no nutritive value and lead to obesity, salt imbalance, and allergies.

David Suzuki

A Mini Cleanse

Detoxifying the body helps optimize brain function and restore the body to its natural state. Unfortunately, many of today's products available at the grocer are riddled with preservatives, nitrates, sodium benzoate, and other toxic additives. A Mini Cleanse is a valuable resource to increase energy levels and rejuvenate a sluggish body. When you stop ingesting chemicals and synthetic over-processed edibles (because they are not really food), your body will begin to flush out toxins. A Mini Cleanse can consist of simply eliminating; dairy, alcohol, and caffeine for a week while increasing your water consumption. You could also do a brief protein and veggie diet, choosing fish and lean poultries over red meat and eliminating simple carbohydrates. A good rule to follow during this practice is to choose foods that were available a century ago. That means nothing that comes in a package or a can. Anytime you give your body a break it allows your organs an opportunity to release build-up, and gives your blood a chance to cleanse, rejuvenating the entire body system. Instead of waiting for the right time to do a full cleanse, try a mini cleanse periodically.

Just because you're not sick doesn't mean you're healthy.

Author Unknown

A Healthy Boost

When looking for a boost – something to get you through the day – often the first options that spring to mind are candy bars and caffeinated beverages. Caffeine provides a temporary lift, only to have your energy level crash shortly thereafter. What you may not know is that caffeine stimulates the fight or flight mechanism in the body by increasing the production of stress hormones. When the body experiences high levels of adrenaline and cortisol, the problem solving area of the brain (the frontal lobe) can shut down. High doses of caffeine and sugar can also lead to panic attacks and dehydration, along with a multitude of other symptoms. Too much of either can speed up your heart rate and raise blood pressure, while slowing down your liver function as your body uses energy in an attempt to assimilate the chemical reaction. Be sure to weigh in on the cost verses benefit of your afternoon boost. Follow the rules of moderation. On any given day, for optimal body chemistry, opt for spring water, fresh veggies, a protein bar, a smoothie, or lean proteins as a way to maintain a steady stream of fuel for the mind and body system.

Why do we alienate ourselves so much from our bodies? It's that big piece of machinery attached to your head.

Carrie Latet

GMO Caution

In an attempt to minimize harvest loss due to insects, scientist created genetically engineered crops that are resistance to pesticide, herbicides, and extreme environmental conditions. The GMO product carries a longer shelf life and often looks flawless, but there is currently widespread concern over the potential side effects of consuming genetically modified living organisms. In Europe, all products containing GMO are required by law to be labeled as such. Commonly modified products include wheat, corn, tomatoes, canola, fish, and soy. Keep in mind that most non-organic meat and dairy producers are fed GMO food, plus steroids and antibiotics. GMOs have been around less than two decades, so until we have a better long-term understanding of the impact of these modified products, it may be best to avoid them altogether and opt for organic non-processed options whenever possible. Beware – there's even orange juice on the market that has fillers of corn and sucrose while claiming to be healthy due to 50% less sugar. Just because it's available does not mean it's been researched and proven safe.

As for butter versus margarine, I trust cows more than chemists.

Joan Dye Gussow

Discover the Source

Our culture has a habit of addressing symptoms and neglecting the source of such. The pharmaceutical industry thrives on this. Take a pill and stop the symptoms − reap the illusion of temporary wellness. Psychiatrists routinely prescribe anti-depressants and sedatives for people going through a divorce or the death of a loved one. Shouldn't they be prescribing yoga and a diet of pure foods? Don't get me wrong − these are by no means easy situations. But they are a normal part of life all the same − things we need to learn to cope with. So many of our societal issues today originate from our propensity to mask the symptom and ignore the root cause of a problem. Have pain? Take a painkiller. A man with a body part that doesn't function? Pop a blue pill. The cause of the dis-ease still exists, but we make ourselves numb to the physical reality of the situation. Consider this: When you transform a negative thought pattern, you are in fact addressing ailments from a cellular level − where they are created. Allow yourself to get to the root. Recognize that in order to heal it, you must be willing to feel it.

Doctors are men who prescribe medicines of which they know little, to cure diseases of which they know less, in human beings of whom they know nothing.

Voltaire

The Invisible World

All I have seen teaches me to trust the Creator for all I have not seen.

Ralph Waldo Emerson

Invisible Barriers

If you were to place a piranha in an aquarium and put a glass partition in the middle, with a goldfish on the other side, you'd witness the piranha instantly become aware of the goldfish and instinctively try to catch it. In fact, the piranha will painfully bump up against the glass repeatedly in a desperate attempt to devour the appetizing fish. After thousands of attempts and a very sore nose, the piranha will learn to give up. In psychology, we call this called *learned helplessness.* Now, after removing the glass partition – shockingly, the piranha will remain on its side of the tank, never crossing the invisible barrier. The piranha will starve to death with lunch right in front of it because it's *certain* it cannot reach the goldfish. The piranha's brain is sending a message that there's a barrier that's impossible pass – after all, that's what it has learned. You have similar barriers, only your glass partition may have been a few failed relationships, a mean teacher, or a well-intentioned Parent God telling you what is or is not possible in your life. Take a moment to consider what your invisible barriers may be and then ask the very important question: What can I do to break free?

History is louder here, almost louder than the present.

Jeremy Taggart

74

The Critical Nature of Focus

When transforming something in your life it is critical that the focus encompass the desired result. Your language choice foreshadows and ultimately predicts the outcome. That being said, if your goal is weight loss and you tell yourself you are *done being fat*, what do you think your mind hears as an outcome? Certainly not healthy living and a toned physique. What about creating wealth? Is it helpful to have a conversation about not being broke? Again, it is all about the focal point. To accumulate wealth one must have abundant conversations about prosperity. We see this in society with counterproductive statements such as "don't drink and drive." Lately there has been a movement to "end bullying." To be effective, we must create children with self-esteem. It's the old pink elephant theory: If someone tells you not to think of a pink elephant, what picture comes up in your mind? Exactly—a pink elephant. Focusing on the desired outcome is an extraordinary tool to execute results. Just be clear the center of attention is placed on the result you want.

When you do the common things in life in an uncommon way,
you will command the attention of the world.

George Washington Carver

Psychic Entanglement

Energy is invisible, and the invisible can have remarkable power whether you believe in it or not. Think oxygen, or gravity – you don't need to see them to know that they are working for you. When you experience intimacy with another person you engage an energetic, psychic exchange. Quantum science refers to this as psychic entanglement. In Indian philosophies, it's described as energy cords connecting the chakra's together. This is wonderful when living in harmony, but when disagreement or severances arise it can be very challenging to separate these invisible ties. The consequence is feeling drained, distracted, and as if your thoughts have been hijacked. Here's what to do: Imagine there's an energy cord connecting you to the person of concern – what would it look like? Why is it there? Now visualize severing that cord using a guillotine, a sword of white light, or an electrical current. Once you've done this, connect your own energy to a positive source. This could be visualizing a tie to the earth for grounding, or perhaps a white light. This exercise will require repetition to successfully disconnect from someone you were once close to.

The evening twilight fades away, the sky is filled with stars, invisible by day.

Henry Wadsworth Longfellow

Animal Totem and Sign

The Native Americans believe that animals show up in our environment to deliver a message. While spending time at my family's beach house, I noticed a goose on the shoreline. He stood out for several reasons. First, he was alone, which is hardly goose-like. Second, he appeared to be staring me down with an attitude. In a moment of curiosity brought on by this creature, I recalled the notion of Animal Totems. Not giving it too much thought, I carried on, only to realize that he was still spying on me an hour later. Looking directly at my goose stalker, I challenged him: "If you really have a message for me, you'll need to do better." I returned with a cup of tea. My goose stalker was now on the back deck glaring in the window, looking directly at my desk two feet away. Impressed with his persistence I threw the phrase "Animal Totem – Goose" into Google, only to find out that the Goose reminds us, among other things, to connect with the written word – precisely the purpose of my trip to the beach house and precisely what I'd been avoiding. If an animal makes its presence known, check and see if it's there to deliver an important message.

It's not what you look at that matters, it's what you see.

Henry David Thoreau

Being Right

You can be right if you like, but keep in mind that being right and being happy...well, they don't always coexist. It's important to evaluate the cost of being right. If you're in a medical environment discussing patient care, "right" is critical. If you're bickering with your partner regarding how late they arrived home last week, is it really necessary to be right? Being "right" often diminishes the person you're making wrong. It's imperative to consider that in many instances more than one person can be right simultaneously – and yes, even on the same topic, due to individual perspectives. For example, if I held up a photograph showing you a picture of a beach ball and asked for a description, the answer would be obvious – a ball with colors, and so on. Now imagine for a moment you're looking at the opposite side of the photograph. You could easily argue that what you are looking at is, in fact, a piece of blank white paper with the word Kodak written on it. In reality, it's the same item, and both viewpoints are valid and accurate from each perspective. Think of this next time you're adamantly defending your view point.

Everything we hear is an opinion, not a fact. Everything we see is a perspective, not the truth.

Marcus Aurelius

Keep Dreaming

As children, many of us are told by the Parent Gods, "You can do anything you want." However, by the time you become a teenager the "be realistic" conversation has hit home. Basically you can do anything you want as long as it involves NOT becoming an actor, inventor, or anything else that sounds risky. There are no benefits to being realistic. In fact, it's a great way to not fulfill – or even touch on – your potential. It sets you up for a life that lacks challenge and excitement. Think about it: If Thomas Edison had been realistic, you just might be reading this book by candlelight. If Alexander Graham Bell was a realist, how do you suppose we'd have been communicating for the past several decades? The truth is, it's not realistic to send a heavy metal cylinder filled with people over the Atlantic Ocean to visit the Eiffel tower. Fortunately, the Wright brothers didn't think this way.

Being realistic is the most common path to mediocrity.

Will Smith

Secret Manifesto List

A well-known Universal Law is the Law of Attraction. This law states that you will ultimately attract that which you place your attention on, either positive or negative. Thomas Troward, a strong influence for the New Thought Movement, said, "The action of Mind plants the nucleus which, if allowed to grow undisturbed, will eventually attract to itself all the conditions necessary for its manifestation in outward visible form." Though not currently considered a science, it has received more and more consideration by credible academics over the past decade. Why not conduct your own personal experiment with the Law of Attraction by making a list of things you would like to manifest and routinely placing attention on them – a Secret Manifesto List. As you manifest different items for yourself and others, you can add new things to the list. Start small, with a cup of coffee or receiving a check in the mail. Gradually you can move on to bigger things – a business partner that shares the same philosophies, or an opportunity for someone you care about. Since this experiment focuses on abundance, you have nothing to lose!

The Law of Attraction states that whatever you focus on, think about, read about, and talk about intensely, you're going to attract more of.

Jack Canfield

Unconscious Triggers

Sandy attended a personal growth seminar and was asked to walk around the room, shake hands with anyone she passed, and state either "I trust you" or "I don't trust you." Sandy had assessed herself as someone who was a trusting individual. The exercise began and she shook hands with one person after another, stating, "I trust you," as instructed. After six people, Sandy approached a young woman whose mannerisms were remarkably similar to her younger sister's. Her sister had a habit of stealing her belongings when they were teenagers. Somewhat surprised, Sandy was apologetic in her approach. "I'm sorry, I don't trust you," she stated to the women. What an eye-opening experience. On Monday, when she returned to her office, Sandy realized that her boss – with whom she bumped heads frequently – also reminded her of her sister. What she had assumed to be intuition was an old trigger. From that moment on, she stopped projecting her distrust of certain personality characteristics that unconsciously reminded her of the past. Sandy quickly garnered an appreciation for her boss and is now able to recognize her many endearing qualities.

The best way to find out if you can trust somebody is to trust them.

Ernest Hemingway

Give Up Knowing

The brain looks to prove what it believes to be true, a considerable limitations of the human race. You think you know how things will work out, and you look for evidence according to your personal history and knowledge. Unfortunately, the phenomenon of memory forces many of us to relive the past over and over again. Some will unconsciously create circumstances and situations to orchestrate the exact experience again and again. The characters may change, but the play is still the same – all to reinforce a belief. Others may pull themselves out of life and stop engaging new experiences because they feel certain of the predicted outcome. This illusion of certainty, tied into deep-seated emotional belief, is the brain's way of protecting itself from perceived future pain. In most cases, the result is in fact the opposite. To find out if an opportunity, person, or new experience is suitable for you, permit yourself to act independent of fear. The truth is, you really won't know what's possible until you put the past behind you and consider that things can absolutely go another way.

The worst thing one can do is not try, to be aware of what one wants to spend years in silent hurt wondering if something could have materialized – never knowing.

Jim Rohn

Be More

Sometimes life presents us with the opportunity to be more – to stretch ourselves. This could show up as a business prospect, a relationship, or a career redirection. I guarantee you that right now there is some area of life where you could step up and create a new outcome independent of past experience. How you manage an opportunity when it's presented is paramount, and literally has the capacity to alter the course of your life dramatically – that is, if you are willing to step outside of whom you know yourself to be. Look for a moment and define what that area is for you. Are you prepared to take action today in a manner that can accomplish an inspired recourse?

He started to sing as he tackled the thing
that couldn't be done, and he did it.

Edgar A. Guest

Who Are You Attracting?

Have you ever noticed how some people date the identical personality type over and over? They appear grossly perplexed as to how they could possibly attract the same characteristics in a partner yet again, neglecting to recognize the common denominator in the equation. They refer to their experience as "bad luck" as a way to avoid responsibility for their choices. They truly believe the people they draw into their lives are random. The people we attract are not random – they are messengers. Human beings unknowingly send out signals that draw in their unconscious match that will reinforce their beliefs about the world. The people in your life that waste your time, drain your energy, or disregard you will continue to show up until you interrupt the pattern. Learn to be responsible for who you attract and know when it's time to say, "Enough is enough!" That's right, you can politely decline associating with people that do not forward your goals or add value to your life. In fact, I highly recommend it.

The law of attraction works unceasingly throughout the universe, and the one great and never changing fact in connection with it is, as we have found, that like attracts like.

Ralph Waldo Trine

Love in Action

The giving of love is an education itself.

Eleanor Roosevelt

You Are that Someone

Driving to yoga recently, I passed a bird sitting in the middle of the road paralyzed in fear. *Someone should do something about that*, I thought. A few miles later I realized I was battling with myself – do I, don't I? I became the observer as information streamed into my consciousness. I recalled someone saying how so many stupid people get hit trying to save animals in traffic. Then it was my mother's voice: "It's too dangerous!" I became acutely aware of what influences my decision – often opinions and external suggestions that are not my own. I let my mind go silent for a moment, when I realized, *I am that someone AND there is a window when I can act.* I turned around wondering if he would still be there – alive – wondering how many other drivers had the same thought or dismissed him as being *just a bird.* I imagined the road clear, a break in traffic long enough for me to pick him up, and miraculously that's exactly what happened. An unexplained break in traffic allowed me to get a blanket from my car and quickly grab Sam the injured Woodpecker. Sam now lives in my backyard, and whenever I him I am reminded, *I am that someone.*

Make a habit of two things: to help; or at least to do no harm.

Hippocrates

YOU Won the Race!

You have graced this beautiful planet, and the fact is that before you were even born you had already overcome insurmountable odds. How typical of you – you have yet to acknowledge your first and greatest achievement of all. Out of 300 million sperm cells, YOU WON the RACE! You didn't for one moment allow the competition to get in the way. You never questioned whether you were good enough, smart enough, or even how you looked along the way. You didn't worry about failure or what the other swimmers would think. Not once did you complain about the crowded, long, dark journey. No, not you – for days, you kept your eye on the egg and swam for your LIFE. Your timing was impeccable and YOU WON the RACE! Now get on with celebrating your life and living true to the CHAMPION that you know you are. Remember all the undeniable qualities that got you here to begin with – they're in your DNA. You're a champion!

Courage is being scared to death...and saddling up anyway.

John Wayne

A Passion Filled Life

At the 2010 winter Olympics a skilled passionate luger lost his life while taking a practice run on what has been referred to as the fastest luging track ever made. I watched in disbelief as I saw him, along with his dreams, fly off the track – knowing instantly that no one could ever survive such a landing. I became very sad for his family – for the loss of a child they were so proud of. Yet, the more I thought about it, the more I began to see it another way. Nodar Kumaritashvili was living his dream. He had become so incredibly adept at his specialty that he was considered one of the best in the world, and was competing against other leaders in his sport at the most prestigious event any athlete could aspire to. This young man's passion and life was honored by tens of millions of people around the world in an outpouring of love, and for a moment he connected the world with reverence. At 21 years of age he had accomplished all of this. Nodar is a role model for a passion filled life. He reminds us of the importance of pursuing our dreams. We are all dying – that's a fact. The question is, if you went tomorrow, like Nodar, would you have truly been living?

No yesterday has ever been wasted for those who give themselves to today.

Brendan Francis

Reverence

I live in a quaint neighborhood; a neighborhood with streetcars, fruit markets, and flower stores on every corner; a location where people walk or ride their bikes to their destination; a community of people that offer a smile and generous "good day" as they pass each other on the street. One afternoon, deep in thought over something I'm sure was nothing in the grand scope of life, I searched for fresh fruits and vegetables at my favorite local market, Sunny's in Roncesvalles Village. It was there I witnessed three tiny sparrows delighting in celebration over a cherry that had fallen from one of the baskets. One at a time they each took a dive at the plump red fruit, followed by a great big nibble from their luscious find. At one point, like a dance, all three sparrows were joyfully pulling this savory cherry in different directions. My world stood still – I reveled in amazement at the simplicity of the moment as I experienced the pure bliss that one succulent cherry could bring to three little sparrows and a Robin.

Gratitude bestows reverence, allowing us to encounter everyday epiphanies,
those transcendent moments of awe that change forever how
we experience life and the world.

John Milton

Encourage Our Future

Parents and teachers are like gods to young people. They hang on to every word, rarely, if ever questioning a message. Young people will inevitably evolve into the limitations or possibilities they are fed. You see, they believe their elders perceptions of them – valid or not. It's imperative that we instill the concept that anything is possible – for their future and for the future of the world. Nobody necessarily believes they are raising or teaching the next Gretzky, Obama, or Winfrey, but somebody is. Somebody is…

As for the future, our task is not to see it but enable it.

Antoine de Saint-Exupery

Little Differences Are Big

One day a man was walking along the beach when he noticed a boy picking something up and gently throwing it into the ocean. Approaching the boy, he asked, "What are you doing?" The youth replied, "Throwing starfish back into the ocean. The surf is up and the tide is going out. If I don't throw them back, they'll die." "Son," the man said, "don't you realize there are miles and miles of beach and hundreds of starfish? You can't make a difference!" After listening politely, the boy bent down, picked up another starfish, and threw it back into the surf. Then, smiling at the man, he said, "I bet I made a difference for that one."

Original Story – By Loren Eiseley

Our prime purpose in this life is to help others. And if you can't help them, at least don't hurt them.

The Dalai Lama

Write a Thank You Note

A little gesture of kindness has the power to make someone's day, including yours. Recently I visited the drive-thru at Starbucks. A familiar voice came through the speaker: "Good morning, welcome to Starbucks; what can I get you today?" It was Jan, who is always pleasant and upbeat. I placed my order, a half caf non-fat latte. "Coming right up, Robin, I'll see you at the window." I was so impressed! Jan has hundreds of customers, and yet she recognized my voice. When I arrived at the window, I made a point of letting her know that it meant something to me. I felt special, appreciated. The simple gesture of using my name personalized the experience – in fact, it made my day such that it inspired me to write this page. It's so easy to voice dissatisfactions and things we are upset about, but what about making a practice of saying thank you and choosing to acknowledge when someone goes the extra mile? Write a letter, send an email, or even jot a message down on a receipt or business card. Let people know when you experience warm fuzzies from their kind actions.

Everyone has an invisible sign hanging from their neck saying, "Make me feel important." Never forget this message when working with people.

Mary Kay Ash

Love in Action

The reason we find babies so cute and loveable is because they're small, helpless, and neutral – much like a pet. Said another way, they are egoless. At birth, newborns are virtually a blank canvas. Slowly they take on the characteristics of their environment and patterns of their Parent Gods, until they are no longer a cute little bundle of joy. In many instances, that small cuddly person has grown into an opinionated, dramatic, tantrum-driven, self-serving, confused human that is simply mirroring what has been denied or modeled for them, day after day. We easily forget that adults were once infants. In my opinion, the people that come across as the most callous are the ones that have endured the most – they're sensitive. They became hard out of self-preservation because they knew but no other way. When you next run into a human being that is abrupt, resigned, or even cruel, have compassion. Remember that person was once a sweet innocent child, whose needs went unmet. What you're witnessing is a survival mechanism born from a lifetime of pain and confusion. Be kind to the three year old in an adult body.

The people who are the hardest to love are the ones who need it the most.

Peaceful Warrior

Apologies

An apology is a means of acknowledging what you missed, or being accountable when perhaps there was a more favorable way to act or be. Not everyone is capable of apologizing. Some people feel very strongly that it's a sign of weakness, and no matter how badly they may feel they may never utter a word of regret. You may find, however, that in the absence of words some apologize with actions. Words are nice to hear, but if the action does not align, the words are empty and void of meaning. In essence, a true apology is expressed by means of behavior. For the people in your life that may not be able to apologize directly with words, look to see if their actions are saying, *Please forgive me, I am sorry.*

Life becomes easier when you accept an apology you never got.

Robert Brault

Wish for People what They Want

Christine was a writer with a lifelong dream of moving to France and purchasing a little 18th century cottage near the sea. Every time she mentioned this, her mother – who likes to control everything – would list all the reasons it was a bad idea and why she should stay in North America. If her mother was able to see past her own feelings, she would have recognized how much this meant to Christine, and that it was the perfect move for her and her life vision. Christine was left feeling divided, as if in some strange way she would have let her mother down if she followed her desires. So she delayed her dreams until someday, hopefully, when she is no longer conflicted and finally grants herself the permission to go for what she truly wants. Wish for people exactly what they want for themselves. Cheer for them, even if it means you'll lose a bit of what you want in the short term. It's one of the most generous gifts you can bestow on another human being.

Every blunder behind us is giving a cheer for us, and only for those who were willing to fail are the dangers and splendours of life.

Carl Sandburg

Crisis Recovery

There are times when happiness is simply not an option as a response. For instance, when someone dies or you lose something that was very dear to you. Telling yourself to "think positive" is futile. There is an emotional release process you must go through that is unavoidable. The best advice I can give during this time is to remember it's a natural part of life. Millions of people before you have gone through a similar experience and gone on to thrive. After the initial shock, it's critical to check in with yourself: Are you staying active, connected, and busy in search of solutions, determined to find the silver lining? Or did you pull a Houdini, looking to instantly escape your reality, numbing yourself and eventually creating more issues than what you were originally faced with? Post crisis, there are actions that support the healing process and behaviors that detract from it. Be wise with choices now more than ever. Far too many people neglect to self-nurture and unconsciously define themselves by a crisis, thwarting opportunities to fully recover. Reach out and get support. Be someone who recovers.

A sad soul can kill you quicker than a germ.

John Steinbeck

Darkness

Darkness is a collection of all the negative patterns of humanity. It's a part of our world and something we can learn from. It scares us so because we all hide some degree or version of darkness within: a selfish act, not considering the feelings of another, a fantasy of revenge, a mind untamed, disregard, cruel intentions, justification, or thoughtless anger. Denying it is pointless, resisting it creates persistence, so let's accept it as part of the collective experience and get busy embracing humanity as a whole. By doing so we can shine light where the world needs it most.

Once asked when she started her work for abandoned children, she replied,
"On the day I discovered I had a little Hitler inside me."

Mother Teresa

Be Kind

Life gets better when you become present to all the characteristics you appreciate in the people around you. What were you originally drawn to in your mate? What wonderful qualities do your family members have when you take the attention away from the attributes you're not fond of? Focus on what you adore about the people in your environment and give up the expectation that they should be infallible, or any other way except exactly how they are right now. This is Love in Action.

There's one sad truth in life I've found while journeying east and west – The only folks we really wound are those we love the best. We flatter those we scarcely know, we please the fleeting guest, and deal full many a thoughtless blow to those who love us best.

Ella Wheeler Wilcox

Logic & Reason

The last function of reason is to recognize that there are an infinity of things which surpass it.

Blaise Pascal

Ask Wise Questions

Whether you ask the question "why me" or "how do I get what I want," your brain will inevitably provide you with a response. It's what the brain does. Successful, happy people spend very little time on problems – they gravitate towards solutions and ask questions of which they *want* to hear the answers.

Successful people ask better questions, and as a result, they get better answers.

Tony Robbins

Fixing & Changing Others

Occasionally we may be inspired to change, perhaps by a life event or the vision of a greater future. But the truth is, for most it is only after significant suffering – seeing the impact of our life choices on ourselves and others – that we finally initiate change. Of course, that doesn't stop us from trying to change our partner, child, friend, or boss. Know this: When you demand someone change, they may temporarily. However, 9 times out of 10 times they will revert back to the old behavior because they haven't learned on an emotional level why they've changed. Though people do change, remember, they do it on their terms – and more often than not, after hitting rock bottom. If you really want to change somebody and be successful, I suggest you pick YOU!

I haven't got the slightest idea how to change people, but I still keep a long list of candidates just in case I should ever figure it out.

David Sedaris

Fashion & Grooming Choices

Your fashion and grooming choices are an important statement constantly communicating to the world how you feel about life and what you expect. Just like a smile or a frown, they say something about your emotional disposition, your habits and preferences. There are common interpretations we have about how people dress that register on an unconscious level. That being said, you can read a lot about a person fairly accurately by how they present themselves. An outfit can express all sorts of things. That ironed shirt says, "I pay attention to details."The person who lives in sweat pants likely puts comfort above all else. A highly visible tattoo may send the message of "notice me" or "I'm a rebel." Some choices scream, "I care, I'm worth it," while others may highlight a dysfunction. That offensively short skirt −to many, it denotes, "I don't value myself." Too much makeup can imply one is wearing a mask, or even "I don't like what I see in the mirror." Grooming makes a statement that others will interpret. Fair or not, people are evaluating you and may choose to listen to you or do business with you simply based on presentation.

Our hearts are drunk with a beauty our eyes could never see.

George W. Russell

You Train How the World Listens to You

How your environment listens to you depends largely in part to your repeated behavior. Think Mother Teresa – what comes to mind? The average response is likely to encompass her saintly generosity and tireless commitment to a noble cause. She unequivocally lived her purpose of helping those in need. Then we have Lindsay Lohan – absolutely talented, yes. However, her repeated actions would lead people to believe she seems to think she's above the law, showing little gratitude for the opportunities presented her. Both earned their reputations by reinforcing a behavior. Now, if either of them had begun to behave differently, it would likely be some time before people could even recognize the new behavior. The past often speaks louder than the present. A history can color the ability of others to witness current action. In other words, if people reliably count on you to be late, you may be early 15 times before they notice. Re-training the listening in your environment takes time, but with patience and commitment it can be done – proving yet again that change is easier than we sometimes believe.

A man's growth is seen in the successive choirs of his friends.

Ralph Waldo Emerson

When Did Chocolate Become a Health Food?

I've seen an awful lot of people devouring chocolate recently, claiming it's a health food, as suggested by the media. So what about chocolate? Chocolate contains cocao, and antioxidants that deliver oxygen to cells. Antioxidants are good for the body, but the sugar and fat found in chocolate contribute to high cholesterol and weight gain, and can strain the liver, among other things. Eating chocolate for the antioxidant content is comparable to drinking soda pop or whiskey and claiming it's a good source of water. Eating blueberries for the antioxidants – now this makes sense. If you've convinced yourself chocolate is part of a health regiment, you will likely gain weight. If your cholesterol and body fat are low and you are free of yeast issues, moderate amounts of 85% cocao organic chocolate may be fine. But don't be fooled by the advertisements, a diamond does not necessarily mean forever, and chocolate is not a health food, as recently implied by the media. But kudos to both of the marketing teams that invented the slogans!

Back in the '70s, 9 out of 10 doctor's recommended smoking. Learn for yourself until you are satisfied you have uncovered the truth.

Robin H-C - Life's in Session!

Monogamy

I have heard the following on more than one occasion from married people: "I don't know that human beings are designed to be with one person." I have a rather simple solution – those who feel this way should not agree to it. There is nothing wrong with being a player when you're straight about it. In fact, it has integrity. We can learn valuable teachings from people like Tiger Woods and Jesse James. A duplicitous lifestyle hurts all parties involved and creates a big mess that can take a lifetime for many to recover from, including children. Being honorable is a choice. A recent study indicates that after our parents, our romantic relationships directly affect and shape who we become in life more than any other. Please – care enough for that person you say you love. Memories cannot be erased and healing deep emotional wounds is an energetic and timely process that requires tremendous fortitude. Not everyone has, or is capable of, this level of healing.

Live so that when your children think of fairness,
caring, and integrity, they think of you.

H. Jackson Brown, Jr.

Meat Free Monday's

I was six years old and thoroughly enjoying a hamburger when my father asked, "How's the cow patty?" "Why did you call it that, Daddy?" "Because hamburgers come from cows," he replied. I immediately began crying, wondering how anyone could hurt such a beautiful creature – in my eyes, a pet. I was confused by the Parent Gods for all they had taught me about right and wrong and do onto others. I became increasingly skeptical. A short time later, my mother served me lunch, encouraging me to eat my asparagus. "Sparrow guts!" I screamed. "You can't make me!" Well, it turns out she could, but that's not the point. From a very young age, I saw beyond societal conditioning. To this day, the idea of ingesting a creature is simply barbaric. A cow is no different than a cat, giraffe, or horse. What is considered acceptable to eat is determined by conditioning and varies from culture to culture. If you were born in Asia, snakes and dogs are popular dishes. In India one does not put ketchup on a sacred cow – one prays to it! I am not asking you to give up meat entirely – simply enjoy a meat-free meal every once in a while, just because.

A man can live and be healthy without killing animals for food; therefore, if he eats meat, he participates in taking animal life merely for the sake of his appetite.

Leo Tolstoy

Manage the Quality of Conversation

Think about it: The quality of conversation you have with yourself on a daily basis determines your life experience. Moment by moment your Internal Broadcaster is assessing and evaluating every person and circumstance you encounter. Though it may not always seem like it, you do have a choice in how you talk to yourself and what you think about. Author Stephen Covey created the 90/10 principle – 10% of life is made up of what happens to you, with the remaining 90% of life being determined by your reaction. Begin to tune into your internal conversations and become aware of what you are saying about what's happening in your life – especially around that uninvited 10%. In the absence of your own positive self talk, get busy connecting with inspiring people or listen to motivational audio books. These simple actions have the power to shift your perception, instill possibility, and assist you in reconnecting with your powerful voice.

The one self- knowledge worth having is to know one's own mind.

Francis H. Bradley

Friendship Divorce

On occasion, it may make sense to divorce people in your life that you weren't ever married to – a friendship divorce. Gabrielle and Faith were best friends for 10 years. Gabby began a path of personal evolution, releasing old patterns and, like many, seeing new possibilities in the process. Faith resisted the changes in Gabby and became annoyed and even critical of her enthusiasm, calling her a dreamer and disputing every idea she passionately shared with her. After many months of frustration and several attempts to have Faith embrace her exciting new journey, Gabby recognized and finally accepted that she was growing in a different direction than Faith, and that for her own well being it was time to let go of the relationship in its current capacity. Though they had shared some wonderful memories, Gabby moved forward and chose to surround herself with nurturing people better aligned with her vision of an inspired future.

Surrounded by people who love life, you love it too;
surrounded by people who don't, you don't.

Mignon McLaughlin

Therapy

I once coached a woman who stated that she had seen more progress with me in three weeks of Coaching than she had in 23 years of psychotherapy. I must admit it was disconcerting to learn anyone would continue to do something for that length of time without seeing substantial progress. By and large, when you make a commitment that every Tuesday at 3:00 pm you'll discuss your greatest disappointments in life, you're placing the past into the present and into the future. Indeed, occasionally it is necessary to diffuse emotions and sort things out, especially after traumatic events. Be cautious though, as conversely, your Tuesday 3:00 pm may have you more identified with your history in the present moment than your current-day life or future. Do refrain from reliving and clinging to past hurts or building an identity around your treacherous life moments. If you are currently in therapy and your doctor agrees, be sure to request time to focus on cathartic practices such as creating, planning, and living an inspiring today and tomorrow. Only you can take the past out of your future.

You can stay in therapy your whole life, but you've got to
live life and not talk about life.

Tracey Gold

Labels

Many years ago, researchers did a study to determine the impact on young people's self-concept by those they view as powerful. Researchers evenly divided 6th graders into two groups, balancing out maturity level, socio-economic backgrounds, intelligence, and ability. One group was told they were gifted, while the other group was told they would find their studies hard and struggle. The students were given identical assignments. After four months, the "gifted" children were thriving. The second group struggled, as they were told they would. A follow-up 10 years later revealed that although the labels had been lifted, the kids deemed "gifted" were still excelling in high school and performing in every area of life – sports, arts, etc., while the kids labeled as "strugglers" were receiving below average grades, scoring lower on intelligence tests, less physically active, and more likely to be in trouble. Both groups accepted their self-concept from their environment and fulfilled on the expectation. Think twice before assigning labels to anyone, and if you do, make sure it's exceedingly positive. – there's a strong chance someone will live into what you tell them they are.

If I accept you as you are, I will make you worse. However, if I treat you as what you are capable of becoming. I help you become that.

Carl Jung

Suicide

It takes a lot of heartache for a person to reach the point where suicide seems like a viable solution to one of life's problems. Someone contemplating suicide has almost always experienced a lifetime of challenges and struggles. Suicide is a thinking issue. Someone in this position feels they have no control over their thoughts. Presumably, they feel powerless to change whatever is going on. The lack of power lives within the Internal Broadcaster and self-conversation. "Nothing ever works out, why bother, I always screw up, people are better off without me." And they believe what they say. Their every perspective is tainted by a defeatist interpretation of a problem. The internal conversation as it relates to challenges takes on a black or white perspective – a victim of one's own thoughts in the most extreme context. One of the unfortunate things about suicide – and there are many – is how the pain is then transferred to the friends and family of the victim, as they are left wondering what, if anything, they could have done.

Someone was hurt before you, wronged before you, hungry before you, frightened before you, beaten before you, humiliated before you, raped before you...yet, someone survived...

Maya Angelou

A Slow-Poke Society

Today, we recognize the Internal Broadcaster as a normal part of cognition. A century ago, any talk of a divided self or hearing voices in your head could land you in an infirmary, possibly undergoing a trans-orbital lobotomy. If you haven't heard of this procedure before, it's where they hammer ice picks through the upper space in the eyelids to disconnect the nerves in the frontal lobe and diffuse emotion. The last one was performed in 1967 by a psychologist with no surgical training – hence the highly technical surgical tools, an ice pick and a hammer. The patient? A young boy whose mother had died. He was acting out after his father's sudden re-marriage. Let's put this into context – this is medicine less than 50 years ago. It just goes to show you how much we've yet to learn culturally. We're accustomed to accepting information from what society deems our "experts," routinely put forth in the media, yet most experts reiterate old information. If something doesn't ring true for you, have the courage to think outside of today. You may become the empirical lead in discovering the genesis of the future – something the world needs more of.

Mankind has survived catastrophes. He will also survive modern medicine.

Gerhard Kocher

Mind Body Spirit

Once we believe in ourselves, we can risk curiosity, wonder, spontaneous delight, or any experience that reveals the human spirit.

E.E Cummings

The Mind & Body

For decades, mainstream medicine has attempted to separate the mind from the body. The body is a system that includes the brain and the mind too. They co-exist, and neither functions very well without the other. If you're a doubter, next time you visit Mexico, drink the water. As your "body" reacts to the foreign bacteria, see how well you're able to focus your thoughts. On the same note, imagine attempting to beat your best running time while processing the death of a loved one. It likely won't happen. When the body goes weak, the mind goes weak; and when the body is strong, the mind often follows. They're not two independents entities, as once thought. It's an interactive system constantly working to co-exist. The Mind and Body are one.

Bodies devoid of mind are as statues in the market place.

Euripides

Love Your Liver

There are few organs in the body as impressive as the liver. The only internal organ capable of regeneration, your liver is responsible for over five hundred vital functions. One of its most significant roles is to process every toxin that enters your system. The liver rids the body of chemicals you inhale from rush hour pollution, air fresheners, cologne — among other unsuspecting pollutants — and topically ingested substances as well. Another important function of the liver is its regulation of hormones, including those released under emotional stress (namely adrenaline and cortisol). In Chinese medicine, the liver is said to be the area of the body that harmonizes emotion and balances energy flow (Qi) throughout the body. It is also commonly referred to as the Seat of Anger. Suffice to say, the liver is an incredible organ and should be nurtured, especially during periods of stress. In Elizabeth Gilbert's book *Eat, Pray, Love,* the Balinese healer speaks about smiling with every part of one's body — especially the liver — with the intention of cleansing and restoring positive Chi to the body.

To meditate only you must smile. Smile with face, smile with mind, and good- energy will come to you and clean away dirty energy. Even smile in your liver. Too serious, will make you sick. You can call the good energy with a smile.

Ketut Liyer

Your Body: a Chemical Rollercoaster

What is your dominant emotion? Are you often angry, confused, or overwhelmed? Scientists have discovered that we have emotional addictions. As such, we create situations and circumstances to fulfill the biochemical needs of the cells of the body. This is an unconscious process that may feel as though it's real and happening to you – and in a way, it is. Pay attention and you'll soon bear witness to the intricate chemical rollercoaster that you are. How do you know it's happening? Say your dominant emotion is anger. When your body is craving anger, it will search your immediate environment to justify the anger. It may sound something like this: "I am angry because my partner doesn't do enough, or because that other driver just cut me off, or my boss was disrespectful!" In the event you cannot find something to blame your emotions on, that may be the moment you stub your toe or spill coffee on your brand new jacket. Bang, just like that – there's the reason for your pissy mood! Yes, you are that complicated! Tune in. Now slowly resist the opportunity to justify that emotion you visit oh so frequently – see how it grows...

*Feelings are much like waves, we can't stop them from coming
but we can choose which one to surf.*

Jonathan Mårtensson

116

Heal Your Body

Do you currently have an ailment? Be it mild or severe, a body that is sick is attempting to wake up the mind to address something critical. Consider that your illness is repressed energy—or, said another way, resistance to a life lesson. When you refuse to forgive or change, your body becomes blocked emotionally, eventually resulting in sickness. The longer you ignore it and act as if it is separate from you, the more acute the illness becomes. Be it pain or disease, it is a reflection of stress levels and an unresolved emotional issue in your life. Try this: Talk to your illness. If there were a reason for it, what might that reason might be? Inquire: What does it need to heal? Or what do you need to let go of, forgive or address for healing to be possible? You could talk to your organ that is under stress and thank it for all it does for you. Many of us are severely disconnected from our bodies and the messages they are constantly communicating to us. It is only when we reconnect and listen that balance can be restored and eventually healing can take place.

Your Body IS your subconscious mind.

Candace Pert

Your Face is Telling You a Story

Body Organ Face Map

Chinese medicine can teach you how to effectively interpret epidermal imperfections. Your skin can provide many clues about an organ under stress based on blemishes or rashes in the face. Similar to reflexology, there is a point on the face for each organ. It is believed that if you experience reoccurring blemishes it is a sign your body is detoxifying the organ that corresponds on the face map. Knowing this allows you to make adjustments to your diet and lifestyle to cleanse or de-stress the organ in question.

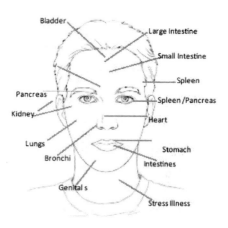

The body is sensitive. It registers every thought and feeling. Be tender with it.

Brendan O'Regan

Nourish Your Mind & Body

When you sit down this evening with your family or dinner guests, ask everyone to share an exciting recent success. Monday's highlight may be attending an exercise class or being kind to someone when it was tempting to act otherwise. Friday's milestone could be an exciting promotion, a team sport well played, or –who knows – you may have experienced the opportunity of a lifetime! The point of this practice is to expand your positive focus and habitually acknowledge affirmative action. Of course, there are many variations of this: what you appreciate about the person sitting next to you; a favorite life moment; people from history you admire; or simply sharing a few thoughts from your Bucket List. Have fun with it and nourish your mind as you nourish your body!

He who loves the world with his body may be entrusted with the empire.

Lao Tzu

Jump-Start Your Immune System

In her book *Molecules of Emotion*, scientist Candace Pert explains how every one of us has several tiny cancerous tumors growing in our bodies at any given time. Fortunately, there's a specific part of the immune system that's designed to kill off these cell before they become large enough to cause illness. According to Stanford researcher David Spiegel, there is an increased rate of survival in cancer patients that express their emotions, including anger and grief. Emotional expression is tied to the natural flow of peptides that support immune function. Candace shares: "Sometimes the biggest impetus to healing can come from jump-starting the immune system with a burst of long suppressed anger. How and where it's expressed is up to you – in a room by yourself, in a group therapy situation where the group dynamic can often facilitate the long buried feelings, or in a spontaneous exchange with a family member or friend. The key is to express it and then let it go, so it doesn't fester, build, or escalate out of control."

Emotion always has its roots in the unconscious and manifests itself in the body.

Irene Claremont de Castillejo

Illness

In the past decade, mainstream medicine has evolved with leaps and bounds, finally recognizing the impact of stress, thoughts, and happiness as a strong component of physical well being (or lack thereof). Consider the fact that almost all illness is psychosomatic. This is good news, in that by acknowledging your thoughts and attitude as a profound contributor to both disease and healing, you are now in control of your physical wellness. Many studies have concluded the impact that both laughter and positive affirmations have on the healing process. The body is a complex living organism that is receiving messages at every moment. Louise Hay authored an incredible book entitled *Heal Your Body, Heal your Life*. If you are struggling with a health issue, I highly recommend taking control of your destiny by exploring the healing practices offered in her book. Doing so means accepting responsibility for every person and situation you have invited into your life or refused to let go. It may sound like a lot, but it's worth it in order to initiate healing.

Healing comes when the individual remembers his or her identity- the purpose chosen in the world of ancestral wisdom- and reconnects with that world of spirit.

Malidoma Patrice Some

The Power of a Thought

Have you ever noticed how a dog responds prior to feeding time? When it sees food, it begins to drool in anticipation of the meal. One thought – "food" – initiates this physical response. You too may have experienced this when reaching for something – perhaps salt and vinegar chips, or sour gums. Your mouth begins to salivate in preparation of the sensory experience. This illustrates exactly how much power one thought can have over the body. As you begin to tune into your thoughts – especially the limiting ones – you'll develop the ability to recognize the physical impact one thought can have throughout your body. In laboratory studies they discovered that one drop of human saliva taken during a time of active fight or flight response and injected into a rat actually kills it in a matter of minutes. Just imagine for a moment the implications that long-term worry and stress can have on your health. There's a reason people die on Mondays more than any other day of the week.

The concept of total wellness recognizes that our every thought, words, and behavior affects our greater health and well-being. And we, in turn, are affected not only emotionally but also physically and spiritually.

Greg Anderson

Acupressure and Your Ears

Following the principles of Chinese medicine, acupressure and acupuncture is the practice of stimulating pressure points to correct imbalances of energy throughout the body, otherwise known as Qi. Acupuncture is the use of tiny needles to stimulate energy, while acupressure is the process of gently squeezing these points. Both result in Qi being drawn to a targeted organ. Your ears reveal the highest concentration of acupuncture points in the body with upwards of 200 targets. The Chinese believe the body creates illness and well-being based on energy flow or stagnation. It is said that simply massaging the ears regularly stimulates energy flow, benefiting your organs and entire body system. You be the judge. Make it part of your practice when you get into bed – or you could add it as a ritual when you're watching television, riding the bus, or waiting for a traffic light to change.

Health is a relationship between you and your body.

Terri Guillemets

Mental Clarity via Cleanse

The average North American diet is loaded with over-processed, nutritionally void foods that strain the liver and toxify the body. In addition to our diet, we also deal with airborne toxins, be they pesticides or other forms of pollution. Make it a habit every few months to engage in a mild cleansing process. For 3–10 days, juice several green vegetables with a lemon. The lemon, which alkalizes in the body, stimulates bile and supports your liver while adding great flavor to a green drink. Snack on celery and cucumber, and have a handful of almonds as a protein source. During any cleanse be sure to drink plenty of water, and if you feel you need something more to eat, have quinoa or brown rice. Remember to ease into it by having light meals and pure foods the days leading up to and following your cleanse. Ideally choose times of low activity. Cleansing is a great way to remove the poisons from your system and to increase energy. Plus, it aids you in suspending the vices that often become dependencies. Expect to feel good and have a positive outlook when the vehicle through which you experience life has been revitalized.

Our bodies are our gardens – our wills are our gardeners.

William Shakespeare

Mind 101

The mind, let's say, is divided into two parts: the conscious and the unconscious. The unconscious controls functions that are involuntary, such as breathing, digesting food, and sending blood flow to your vital organs – all of which take place without thought. You do not need to remind yourself to breathe. Similar to a machine, your body automatically knows to do this. The unconscious also holds all of your beliefs about yourself and the world around you, and acts as a matrix creating the context of what's possible for you in your life. Beliefs are imprinted by our thoughts and interpretations of our environment, and created when the mind accepts information given to it in a state of heightened emotion and repetition. It carries no concept of time and, much like a DVD, it replays whatever it has stored. Therefore, if at six years of age events led you to tell yourself, "I always mess things up," and your mind accepted this and replayed that recording over the years – chances are that that six-year-old is still governing some parts of your life today. Yikes!

The human brain is the most complicated
organization of matter that we know.

Jim Rohn

Organs and Their Time of Day

There's an infinite intelligence within the human body that we cannot begin to comprehend. According to Chinese medicine, the life force in the body takes place for different organs at varying times on a 24-hour clock. If you routinely feel sluggish at a certain time of day, or wake up in the middle of the night consistently, check with the chart – you may have an organ under stress. It also follows that healing rituals are best aligned with the organ's life force timing whenever possible.

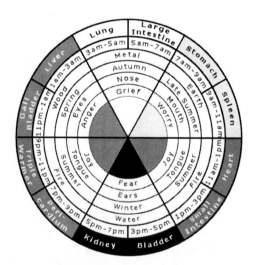

Every human being is the author of his own health or disease.

Buddha

Mysteries & Interesting Facts

Somewhere, something incredible is waiting to be known.

Carl Sagan

Gravity Unleashed

Years ago, in the days of Columbus and Galileo, people believed the world was flat. In fact, they were certain of this. It existed as a reality in the world through agreement. Of course, at that time physicist Sir Isaac Newton had not been hit on the head with an apple, (which impelled his three laws of universal motion, which subsequently led to the discovery of gravity). Without this fundamental understanding, how could the world possibly be round? Until gravity was discovered, it was absurd to surmise the world could be anything but flat because people knew what they knew. Knowledge in this case limited what they saw as truth. Consider: Metaphorically, we have yet to discover gravity and so much more that can explain many of the fascinating capabilities of the human brain and of our world. Keep an open mind. You, me, us – we know virtually nothing, and it's OKAY that we know nothing.

If I have seen further than others, it is by standing upon the shoulders of giants.

Isaac Newton

Mercury Retrograde

Okay, now before you roll your eyes, listen carefully with an open mind. According to astrology, Mercury is the planet that rules communication. Every few months it spins in the opposite direction for several weeks. Astrologers refer to this as a retrograde. It has been recorded during such times that both people and machinery seemed to be heavily influenced by this planetary shift. Much like during a full moon, there is an increase in the number of accidents– hospital visits multiply, machines go kaput, emails bounce back, cars breakdown, and most notably communication issues arise between people. If you consider how we're influenced by weather and other atmospheric conditions, it would only stand to reason that this too can influence human behavior. During a Mercury Retrograde, be flexible with people in your life, as they may not be communicating at their very best. And though it is advisable to *not* make any major life decisions at this time, don't hide in your basement just yet – a retrograde is a favorable time to complete projects you have already started, begin research and reflect on plans for the future.

I don't believe in astrology; I'm a Sagittarius and we're skeptical.

Arthur C. Clarke

Dream Detective

What are your dreams telling you? For decades, scientists and psychologist have strived to provide an answer to this mystery. Imagine your dreams are your unconscious communicating with you. It's as if your unconscious is providing you with a clue to decipher. Many dreams can be interpreted by simply asking yourself what the symbol in your dream means to you, and then examining the emotional tone of the dream. Recurring dreams seem to imply the unconscious need to work through a particular issue – in other words, the brain is attempting to process information and make sense of an experience. Make a practice of recording your dreams and interpreting the message. Look to see if after a few weeks you can successfully decipher the message your unconscious is communication to you.

> *I slept and dreamt life was a joy. I awoke and saw life was service.*
> *I acted and behold, service was a joy.*
>
> *Rabindramath Tagore*

Intention + Action = Synchronicity

It's the easiest thing in the world to talk about the changes you plan to make. But what are you really actively doing to make things happen? Breakthrough results show up the moment you are willing to take extreme action for a cause. When daily actions are aligned with noble intentions, what some may call miraculous results surface almost instantly – and not always from a predictable source. You may begin to make cold calls for your new business and out of the blue an old contact calls with a strong lead. Two days later you are officially in business. Fed up with yourself, on Monday you chop up your credit cards and start looking for a second job to get out of debt. A few days later, your parents, whom you'd never asked a penny from, offer you an interest free loan. Maybe you begin your new healthy lifestyle with a vegetable juice cleanse and walking, only to realize you have lost four pounds by the end of the week. Action coupled with intention is an undeniable combination.

*Whether we name divine presence synchronicity, serendipity, or graced moment
matters little. What matters is the reality that our hearts
have been understood. Nothing is as real as a
magic which restores our spirits.*

Nancy Long

Birthdays

Aging is a funny thing. When we're young, we desperately want to be old for what it can mean for our lives. Recently, when spending time with my adorable little niece Abby, I asked her age. Her response, which of course I knew: "three." "Wow, three! Such a big girl," I said. And with the energy and passion of a ticked off three-year-old, she quickly corrected me, "No, still three!" She then went on to ask me if turning four would mean she could finally drive a car like Mommy and Daddy. When we're young. we want to be older – being a few years older appears like the ultimate. As we age, we tend to want to turn back the hands of time and wish we had appreciated our youth a bit more. Ultimately, birthdays become a barometer for what we want to do or wish we had done. The fact is, when we wish to be any age but what we are, we deny the current moment and potentially block joy by thinking some future or past moment is somehow better than the very moment of now.

In childhood, we yearn to be grown-ups. In old age, we yearn to be kids.
It just seems that all would be wonderful if we didn't have to
celebrate our birthdays in chronological order.

Robert Brault

Death

The response to and interpretation of death varies globally. Hindus, for example, consider death a process of moving to the next life in search of Nirvana through re-birth. The Egyptians, on the other hand, were buried with their most treasured possessions in preparation for the afterlife. Some of them even brought along their servants! Death is subject to the interpretation of the culture you were born into. In North America, when a person passes before their eighth or ninth decade we tend to resist it. It shouldn't be − it's not fair. We humans believe we have answers, and answers − or the illusion thereof − give us great comfort. We have no answer for death, and yet we all accept it as a natural part of the life cycle. On a fundamental level, most of us struggle with death because it reminds us of how little we actually know about life. Honoring every moment − every precious person − and leaving nothing unsaid or undone can alleviate the lack of understanding when we lose someone. Tell someone how you feel today − how knowing them has touched your life.

Religion is the human response to being alive and having to die.

F. Forrester Church

Fact or Opinion?

People speak from their own experiences, opinions, and beliefs, so be careful what you "deem" to be true. Many of us walk around vulnerable to the suggestions of others – suggestions that we far too often give credence too. At an audition at the age of 39, a funny redhead was told by a prominent producer not only that she could not act, but that she was painful to watch. I believe the advice was, "Stop acting, you're not good at it." Less than two years later, Lucille Ball had her own TV show. Eventually she became a Hollywood legend. Had she accepted that producer's opinion, she would have thrown in the towel and the world would have been deprived of a delightful comedian. Become conscious of what you accept into your world as truth. Learn to challenge information. Is it fact or opinion? If it's fact, can the facts be changed? It was a fact that space travel was not possible when John F. Kennedy declared the United States would put a man on the moon. He subsequently changed the facts when he gathered a team of scientists to create the metal to withstand re-entry, thus making space travel possible – which today, of course, is a fact.

Facts and truth really don't have much to do with each other.

William Faulkner

Fight or Flight Response

When human beings feel threatened, our tiny but powerful adrenal glands release a teaspoon of adrenaline. This powerful chemical sends a message to the brain to increase blood flow to the lungs, arms, and legs. It also restricts flow to what it considers the non-essential areas of the body. Can you guess what areas are considered non-essential? You got it: the brain! Specifically, the frontal lobe – the very part we rely on for problem solving. Of course, if you happen to encounter a black bear, this extra blood flow can be very helpful when you need to RUN for your life! The quandary nowadays is that this archaic and primitive reflex is frequently triggered in humans when they feel emotionally threatened. As this happens, many of us forget that our intention was to reach a solution or try to better understand our partner, boss, or friend. You'll know when this occurs because there is a shift from communication to the urge to pull out your verbal warfare and attack. STOP! You are not thinking clearly. Breathe in deeply. Exhale and repeat until you reach a state where you are unequivocally certain blood flow has resumed to your vital areas.

What you do speaks so loud that I cannot hear what you say.

Ralph Waldo Emerson

Words

The process of acquiring language does not involve looking up each word for an exact definition. Even if it did, words are still subject to varying interpretation. It's no surprise that miscommunications are so frequent when the words that we use mean different things to different people. For example the word "transparent," which means both "invisible" and "obvious." Or "fresh" – another word with multiple meanings. There are words that people learn believing they have particular definitions when in fact they mean something else. Language is a tool to understand and be understood, so do your best to be precise when you are speaking – especially with conversations of a critical nature. If you are unsure in a conversation, ask whomever you're speaking with what their definition of a word is, or request that they clarify their message. After all, a word typed into a thesaurus will bring up multiple definitions, but it does not guarantee that any of those definitions fit precisely what you are attempting to articulate.

The single biggest problem in communication is the illusion it has taken place.

George Bernard Shaw

The Happiness Dilemma

It's human nature to be dissatisfied. That being said, you'll have moments that feel complete – even perfect. Then eventually you'll have the experience of un-fulfillment once again. A phenomenon of being human is that most of us operate as though happiness is governed by an external event, an accomplishment or milestone. When that episode passes, changes, or becomes familiar, boredom kicks in. Then you decide something else will complete you. It may sound like this: "Something's missing...if only I had a more money, a better partner, a bigger house, a baby, a designer purse, a Pucci, a Gucci, a Rolex – then I'd really be happy." And you would be, momentarily. Then, once again the excitement of that new shiny thing would inevitably wear off – it always does. In fact, that thing that was once the answer to your happiness over time can turn into a problem – a big problem. Your cute little baby grows into a defiant teenager, your house loses its value, your spouse becomes the size of Shamu, or worse – cheats! And once again you'll seek and eventually find another short-term answer for your current happiness dilemma.

He who has so little knowledge of human nature as to seek happiness by changing anything but his own disposition will waste his life in fruitless efforts.

Samuel Johnson

The Bumble Bee Philosophy

After much study, our brilliant scientists determined that, aerodynamically speaking, the bumblebee cannot fly. If the bee were human, it would probably stop flying because it was told it was not capable. Consider: We are conditioned to believe what is possible for us and the world, when in reality the magnitude of what's truly available to us is beyond our current realm of thinking. Pursue your own greatness. Trust yourself and your intuitions. Immerse yourself in the mystery of life to reach new pinnacles of self. Courageously pursue your wildest dreams and begin to explore who you can be without constraints from the past. If you doubt one person can make a difference in this world, I have one word for you – Gandhi .

However far modern science and techniques have fallen short of their inherent possibilities, they have taught mankind at least one lesson: Nothing is impossible.

Lewis Mumford

People Power

If you want to travel fast ... travel alone ...
If you want to travel far ... travel together ...

African proverb

Become a People Cheerleader!

It's truly astonishing the development a baby undergoes in its first few years of life. Think of a toddler taking his first steps: Wobbly and uncertain, he marches forward, beaming with pride. One step...two steps. "You can do it, baby!" We're encouraging and enthusiastic, pure love in anticipation of his pending accomplishment. It's a major milestone for those little legs; a celebration of life to bear witness to such an ordinary yet miraculous event. Now, imagine if that tiny person took two steps and fell on his behind, and we said, "Ah well, you failed. You fell when you were supposed to walk. Perhaps you should give up and just crawl forever. No, don't try again – you'll never be a walker. In fact, you don't even crawl that well to begin with – you only use one arm!" Can you imagine? Yet as we age we tend to do this with ourselves and others. Become a people cheerleader, an inspiring source of support for not only yourself, but those around you too.

Act as though what you do makes a difference. It does.

William James

Watch People Come ALIVE

So you're talking to someone, say at the office or a social gathering – what could be considered a boring conversation. The weather, the local news, basic surface level cocktail chatter. Likely the commentary in your head is far more entertaining than the conversation you're having. What to do? Take the lead. When you engage a person in a conversation about their passions, people literally come to life in front of your very eyes. Someone you may have considered unattractive can become rather stunning the moment they're talking about what they love most in life. So ask people about their passions, their children, their favorite pastimes or what they'd put on their Bucket List if they have one. This is a magical metamorphosis to witness, it's as if you've pressed the happy button on another human being and you get the honor of watching them come ALIVE!

There are no passengers on Spaceship Earth. We are all crew.

Marshall McLuhan

Learn People's Names

People love to hear the sound of their own name. A small thing in connecting with others, everywhere, is taking the time to learn people's names. It makes interactions feel personal, and it honestly doesn't matter if you'll ever see them again. When you visit a restaurant your server becomes a part of your life experience, and you theirs – even if only for 30 minutes. The cashier at the grocery store has a name, and saying a simple "Hello Linda," can bring a moment of reverence to both of your lives. We really don't know what others are struggling with in life. This simple gesture of kindness has the power to shift perspective and ignite the love for humanity that exists within all of us. It's a small thing that makes a big difference – it shows you care. Every day there are countless opportunities to touch the lives of those we share the planet with. I challenge you to experiment with and embrace this practice of honoring others.

Live in such a way that you would not be ashamed to sell your parrot to the town gossip.

Will Rogers

Circumstances Change with Attitude

Whatever your current life scenario is, it's critical to remember that circumstances are not who you are. Though they can define you, this is only so with your permission. Think of all the incredible stories of people who have succeeded despite insurmountable odds. Mark Ingles, for example, lost both his legs due to frostbite after being stranded in an ice cave for two weeks while mountain climbing in 1982. In 2006, he became the first double amputee to reach the summit of Mt. Everest. He refused to give up in spite of circumstances. Here's a man who accomplished something most able-bodied people would consider impossible. At no point did he empower a conversation such as, "Life's not fair, this is too hard." Absolutely determined, he just got on with it. Use this example to re-evaluate situations in your own life and potentially re-frame them. Let go of any drama surrounding what you're up against to adopt a perspective that allows victory to triumph. Be it a divorce, an illness, a financial meltdown – all of these things can overcome, especially when you realize through placement of attention that they are all in fact temporary states.

I know of no higher fortitude than stubbornness in the face of overwhelming odds.

Louis Nizer

The Inspiring People Poll

If you were to conduct a poll to evaluate the positive people influences in your life, how would you do? Take a moment and reflect on some of your relationships over the years. The people you invite into your life (intentionally or not) have a significant influence on the level of joy you experience and the type of person you evolve into. With some, doors open to offer you an exciting new direction in business or perhaps partnership as a parent. With others, you learn to believe in new possibilities – maybe the dream of a new career or the possibility of love. At the same time, certain interactions may have you ceasing to believe in something you once felt possible. All of your relationships, coupled with your response to them, have helped shape your life and personality into what it is today. Quite frankly, people can make or break a life – especially when it comes to partners. Learn to be selective with your people choices. Do your best to cultivate nurturing, supportive relationships. Have the foresight to gravitate toward inspiring people who will help make your life a delight!

There are souls in this world which have the gift of finding joy
everywhere and of leaving it behind them when they go.

Frederick Faber

Start a Mastermind Group

In my first Mastermind Group, we had Gary the Ph.D., Warren the entrepreneur, me, and Karen the schoolteacher. The objective of such a group is to gather a diverse range of thinkers, to utilize one another as a resource for fresh ideas, and to execute results. Depending on the number of members, 20–30 minutes is allocated for your idea or goal. One at a time, each participant briefly shares their personal or business goals, and the remainder of the time is spent brainstorming on strategies to execute outcomes. Another purpose of a Mastermind Group is to hold you accountable for critical action steps (CAS). It's less likely you'll procrastinate when you answer to other people – which can be incredibly instrumental when expediting results. You can thank your ego for this one!

No two minds ever come together without thereby creating a third, invisible intangible force, which may be likened to a third mind.

Napoleon Hill

Consider Your Impact

In December 1955, Rosa Parks, exhausted from a long day at work, refused to give up her seat on the bus to a white passenger. This single act of courage led to the disintegration of institutionalized segregation in the south, ultimately resulting in a new era of civil rights. Consider a few of the choices you've made in your own life and the impact they've had on you and those around you. Not all of your life choices will have such a profound impact, but some may – especially if you're a parent or a teacher. Bobby, for example, reluctantly took a personal development course at the age of 30. After noticing a shift in her, one by one, her family members were inspired to do the same program. Eventually, several of her friends, clients, and neighbors did too. Within a few months, she became an agent for change facilitating programs on personal power for struggling youth. Thousands of lives were altered, all stemming from one choice to take a three-day introspective seminar that didn't even seem like a great idea at the time! Just one action, however huge or seemingly insignificant, can have a domino effect in the world.

Time is the coin of life. Only you can determine how it will be spent.

Carl Sandburg

Get to Know Your Parents

Funny, I always looked at my parents and assumed their lives began the year I was born. I'd conveniently forgotten they had a whole life before my siblings and I entered the picture. How well do you know the people that gave you life? If you're like most, not as well as you could. I know – no parent is perfect, and neither were theirs, but they did their best, and frankly they're the only parents you will ever have. Why not get to know your parents outside of your current relationship? Ask questions. Inquire as to whom they were before you and your siblings came into the picture. Discover their passions and joys when they were young. Find out what their defining life moments were. What are some of their most indelible memories and hardships that shaped their characters? As you ask questions, you may find you'll discover a whole other side to the person you thought you knew so well. Ask today – there will be a day when you no longer have the opportunity to get to know the people who gifted you life.

Making the decision to have a child is momentous. It is to decide forever to have your heart go walking around outside your body.

Elizabeth Stone

147

What About Anger?

Anger can be a powerful tool. When re-directed, it can take on a new form and aid in healing. There's nothing wrong with anger – the key is to control where and how it's expressed. Don't waste it on strangers on the highway. Have it be worth the life energy you give to it – get so angry you become a voice for change. John Walsh is an extraordinary example of channeled anger. He started the TV series *America's Most Wanted* after his son was abducted. Here's a man that could have curled up on the couch forever with a bottle of vodka forever and been justified in doing so. Instead of allowing his pain to direct him, he put his son's memory and the well-being of other children above all else. He and his wife became a two-person army for missing and exploited children. Despite bureaucratic and legislative challenges, he got angry and active enough that the Missing Children Act of 1982 was finally established. *American's Most Wanted* has subsequently caught over 1000 fugitives and educated parents globally. Walsh gave his son the ultimately legacy when he vowed his life would not be in vain. This is a productive and cathartic use of anger.

The world needs anger. The world continues to allow evil because it isn't angry enough.

Bede Jarrett

Applaud People

I was dining on a patio with a group recently. During the meal, my friends and I engaged in a favorite pastime of people watching. Many people passed our view from the restaurant, including a few runners going on their daily jog. One in particular stood out for her enthusiasm – she weighed about 220 pounds. One of the ladies at the table made a comment about her weight. "I'd never wear that if I was her size – she doesn't even look like she exercises!" Another diner retorted, "For all you know she may have weighed twice that a year ago...good for her!" This opened up a very inspiring discussion on people and where they are on their life journey. It's important to recognize that progress and accomplishment come in varying forms. Without knowing someone's life experience, what you may see as failure could very well be the greatest breakthrough of their life to date. The lady we witnessed jogging may be thrilled with her size 12 after being a size 18 most of her life. Remember, when you look you are only seeing a portion of the picture interpreted through your own subjective filter of the world. There is always more to the story.

Progress lies not in enhancing what is, but in advancing toward what will be.

Khalil Gibran

Create a Team

Anything you want for your life IS possible, and even more so when you design a team of people to help propel forward. Your health team may include a personal trainer and a naturopath. Your business team may have a mentor, or a consultant – possibly both. For your relationship, perhaps ask for help from a couple with a thriving marriage. The Buddhist Centre or a local church may be where you look to build a team to bring spirituality to your life. If you have financial resources, you're in great shape – hire lots of smart people to help you fulfill your intentions. Limited financial resources, or just plain frugal? Don't give up just yet. You have the task of becoming creative while establishing your team. Put together a Mastermind Group. Do a service exchange or find a life coach who is still in training. Enroll a buddy or a partner in your vision. The goal is to gain access to a group of people that will lead you to resources and encourage or nudge you in the right direction in the event that you waver from your ultimate vision. You can design a team for renovating your house, finding romance, or anything else you can dream up for that matter!

When asked why he had a team of 21 assistants...
"If I could solve all the problems myself, I would."

Thomas Edison

Powerful Practices & Habits

*First comes thought; then organization of that thought, into ideas and plans;
then transformation of those plans into reality. The beginning,
as you will observe, is in your imagination.*

Napoleon Hill

The 30–Day Success Diet

What if, for 30 days, you became conscious of your actions? What if, for 30 days, you enthusiastically gave up the things that you know DON'T work for your life – even just some of the time? What if, during those 30 days, you did more of the things you know DO work for your life? And what if, after 30 days, you realized you had FUN challenging yourself, and learned it was far easier than you ever thought possible?

To be able to ask a question clearly is two-thirds of the way to getting it answered.

John Ruskin

Go Direct

If you have something to say to a person in your life that's of a sensitive nature, go direct. Don't be one of those people that airs their complaint to everyone they know – except the one person who can address it. Not only is this undermining, but it creates unnecessary drama and stress for others. Spare your inner circle from feeling the need to take sides. Eliminate the "he said, she said," along with gossip and other problems associated with second-hand information being passed along. If you truly care to resolve the problem – and deep down, I believe you do – going direct is the way to do it. It demonstrates respect and is a mature, solution-based approach to voicing a complaint you have with another.

I'm a great believer that any tool that enhances communication has profound effects in terms of how people can learn from each other, and how they can achieve the kind of freedoms that they're interested in.

Bill Gates

Mind Your Airtime

What's getting airtime in your head? Do you spend time ruminating on your weaknesses, people you have no respect for, and all the things that frustrate the heck out of you? Wasting precious thought energy is a crazy thing to do, but we all do it at times. Think about it: We have 86,400 seconds each day. That's 1440 minutes. Start to become aware of what you allow to consume your delicate headspace. Keep in mind that you're constantly training your body to expect more of the emotional state you frequent. Situations that bring up unfavorable states CAN be interrupted. Make a point of daydreaming about favorable life outcomes that you WANT to experience, like winning a Noble Peace Prize, starting your own business, or renewing your wedding vows.

Every day we touch what is wrong, and, as a result, we are becoming less and less healthy. That is why we have to learn to practice touching what is not wrong —inside us and around us. When we get in touch with our eyes, our heart, our liver, our breathing, and our non-toothache and really enjoy them we see that the conditions for peace and happiness are already present.

Thich Nhat Hanh

Preserve the Listening of Others

Have you ever been frustrated with your partner, friend, or family member? You call someone in a moment of anger to vent your grievance. Human nature takes over, and you're now on a mission to slander this person and convince whoever's listening that your mother, best friend, or spouse is the most insensitive, unbalanced jerk in the world. Oh yeah, and you'll likely never speak to them again – at least for the next few hours anyway. Though venting is necessary at times, having someone agree that the person you're having a falling out with is the biggest creep on the planet isn't. Put the situation into context. In all probability, you'll eventually resolve the issues. But the residual impact of the hate-on you've created – in the event you were successful – can make the next dinner party or family gathering awkward, to say the least. Vent when you need to, but keep in mind the cost of completely slandering a person who is not there to represent their side of the story. The person lending an ear may hold a grudge long after you've let it go. Learn to vent in private – on shreddable, flammable paper – and seek support for solutions publically.

Anger and blaming others takes a lot of energy away from healing. One of the most powerful emotions that has to be expressed is forgiveness.

Candice Pert

155

Give up Your Best – for a Good Job

If you're anything like me, you were raised being told to "always do you best" – a lovely sentiment indeed. Doing your best is a great theoretical approach to life, but not necessarily rational. As a writer, when I review something I've written there is always an urge to make adjustments – it's never ending. If I didn't choose to be finished, my first book wouldn't be complete until I was on my death bed. That would be my best! To do my best each time I run would mean beating my last running time. If I did my best with my diet every day, I would never each cheese or simple carbohydrates, and wine would certainly be out of the question. Not to mention, my best would involve creating a new menu at every meal and growing my own organic vegetables. Get it? So, if you're someone who procrastinates with the concern of achieving perfection or doing your best, stop it! Be satisfied with a job you're proud of, a job well done, a great effort. Too often, best and perfect thwart out intentions and get in the way of living.

You don't have to get it perfect, you just have to get it going. Babies don't walk the first time they try, but eventually they get it right.

Jack Canfield

Your Mood is Contagious

Carl Jung, one of the grandfathers of psychology, wrote many years ago that emotions are contagious. Similar to an airborne virus, some of us are more susceptible than others at varying times, depending on our physical and psychological immunity. Science shows us that a newborn baby will take on the emotions of the mother, happy or sad. It's important to that recognize people unconsciously synchronize their moods – instantly picking up on the unspoken emotions and body language of the people in their environment – especially those they are closest to. With this in mind, people that are highly enthusiastic are liable to evoke a euphoric mood in you, while the opposite is true for time spent with dissatisfied or grumpy individuals. When possible, develop the foresight to seek out company that is adept with harmonious modes of expression that set an undertone of reverence for yourself and your life.

The best way to knock the chip off your neighbor's
shoulde is to pat him on the back.

Author Unknown

Electromagnetic Imprints

If you visualize an outcome, your brain undergoes electromagnetic changes as if you were actually doing the task. Because your brain works on pictures, each time you re-visit a vision you strengthen it. Practice this and your unconscious will send you ideas to execute on any strongly imprinted vision. This is why rehearsing an event (a speech or a sport) in your mind's eye can have the same benefit as an actual physical rehearsal. The brain cannot distinguish between real and imagined. Though your mind may recognize it's your imagination, the body's chemical reaction is identical to the reaction that occurs when it is in fact happening. To enhance the this exercise create a movie screen in your mind with a life-size image of what you want to create in your own personal theater. Add vibrant colors. Watch the image grow. See what you are wearing when you sign that big contract. Identify what you are feeling as if it's actually happening. Hear what you're saying to yourself as you cash that massive check. "I knew this would work!" Get vivid to expedite your results!

Stamp indelibly on your mind a mental picture of yourself as succeeding. Hold this picture tenaciously. Never permit it to fade. Your mind will seek to develop the picture...

Norman Vincent Peale

Highlight Strengths

We live in a somewhat misguided society and most of us grew up hearing where we fell short. As such, our thinking is set up in a similar manner. You may be acutely aware of the areas where you don't measure up, all the while quickly dismissing your notable achievements and many strengths of character. This is part of the human condition, and is also true of the people around you. So keep this in mind during your daily interactions. At the end of the day – or beginning, for that matter – people need to hear what they're doing right. Tell those in your environment everything you appreciate about them. Use verbal feedback to reinforce positive interactions. When addressing things that don't work, always speak from the context of what could work. Learn to be generous and acknowledge the qualities you admire in another human being.

Anywhere you go liking everyone, everyone will be likeable.

Mignon McLaughlin

Connect with Nature

It may not be an African safari this year, but it could be a trip to the zoo or a lakeside picnic. You might connect with the elements by sailing, or simply enjoy the view from your chaise lounge while listening to the sound of the trees. You could meditate on the beach. The wide open space will instantly challenge any heaviness you are carrying and can be the perfect place to release, cleanse, and revitalize. Make it part of your routine to find different ways to connect with nature. Dip your toes in the ocean or take a walk barefoot and feel the earth dance underneath your toes. Our bodies require contact with terrain and all that is natural. Lie down on the ground and appreciate the moving picture of the clouds and sun that no painting could possibly ever rival.

Man must feel the earth to know himself and recognize his values ...
life is simple. It is man who complicates it.

Charles A. Lindbergh

Juxtapose in Both Directions

If you're in the habit of comparing yourself to your neighbors and acquaintances, I have a question for you: Have you taken a moment to look both ways? When you admire other people's successes or observe how lucky someone is, you may want to consider the other side of the equation. There are most certainly people who have far less than you do. Presence yourself to this – it's humbling. If you compare your situation to someone who's achieved more, it can activate a self-deprecating mental state, a focus on the lack. I promise you, there will always be people with more than you, and many with less. In moments when you're tempted to compare, why not direct the comparison within and distinguish just how far you've come? What have you quit, started, or changed in recent years? What characteristics have you developed that have made you a more kind, generous, or entertaining spirit? By comparing both ways or simply measuring by your own progress, an abundance perspective can arise.

He is a wise man who does not grieve for the things which
he has not, but rejoices for those which he has.

Epictetus

Un-Justify for Change

Think of a current condition in your life – something you'd like to change. Now answer the question: What's the reason for this circumstance in my life? Consider: What you believe to be the reason is likely a justification, not the actual reason. It's a pretense. It's simply what you say to yourself to keep your circumstance in place to reinforce an identity. When you change the reason, you change the outcome. If your reason relates to someone else's influence or behaviors, you have trapped yourself and made yourself a victim – and how much power do victims have? That's right – NONE. If you're ready to own your power, change the circumstance by inventing a new reason. One that connects you to a source of possibility.

Change is not merely necessary to life – it is life.

Alvin Toffler

Raising Little Adults

It is easier to build strong children than to repair broken men.

Frederick Douglass

163

Teach your Child to be a Free Thinker

Ask your child for her opinion on a range of topics and validate her perspective. Appropriate responses may sound like this: *interesting, fantastic, how did you think of that?* As you do this, note: You are not to evaluate whether the opinion is right or wrong, or even consistent with your own beliefs. Rather, help her to become fluent in her own opinions, beliefs, and views of the world. Doing so illustrates respect and sends the message that not only is she supported, but that it's safe for her to express her beliefs. When a child has an early neural pattern (brain pattern) that says, "I'm valued," it cultivates a healthy self-concept to build upon. It also reinforces the ability to embrace a range of diverse views, which translates into respect for other cultures, religions, and humanity in general. If she is not able to do this in the security of her own environment, it is unlikely she will ever feel comfortable having a voice in the world. Make sure your children learn they have something to contribute to the world, because they do – yes, even at four years of age.

If you begin with the end in mind, you are in fact raising adults, not children.

Author Unknown

Ask for Feedback

Your child is brilliant and sees and feels everything going on in his environment. Partner with him in your parenting and let him know his voice counts. Interview your child periodically and ask what works and what doesn't work about your parenting. You will need to allow freedom of expression and to be okay with any response the child gives you without correcting or influencing anything that was said. Remember, whatever is offered is the truth in their world, as it occurs to them. Like all people, children are entitled to their perspectives. At a later time you can revisit and say, "how am I doing with xxx?" Your child will enthusiastically offer you a progress report and learn their opinion matters.

Each day of our lives we make deposits in the memory banks of our children.

Charles R. Swindoll

Help Them Earn

Be it a lemonade stand, a garage sale, walking a neighbor's dog, a part-time babysitting gig, or yard work. -The pride and freedom that comes with earning helps children become acquainted with generating revenue long before it becomes a necessity. It creates a sense of independence and control over their life. A young mind that can see earning as fun and playful will likely build on that and enjoy a long, rewarding career with various revenue streams. And just think — in the future this may present as the difference between you living in a retirement home or settling in with care in the west wing of your grown child's estate!

We worry about what a child will become tomorrow,
yet we forget that he is someone today.

Stacia Tauscher

Lessons from a Three-Year-Old

Several years ago my three-year-old nephew Hayden paid me a visit. As he walked in the door he ran over to me and said with enthusiasm, "Auntie me Pish died." He was referring to his goldfish that had passed the day before. My immediate reaction was to say, "Oh Hayden, you must be sad." Realizing that he may have no understanding of death and how society relates to it, it occurred to me that he might not be sad at all. Given that children take cues from adults on how to behave, I recognized that the mere mention of sadness could shape the experience for him. I paused pensively before I spoke. "How was that for you, Hayden?" Hayden responded, "Goog, me got new Pish and new Pish swim more, Auntie!" "Wow, fantastic Hayden." This interaction taught me to inquire instead of assume what a child may be thinking or feeling. As adults, we have a tendency to tell rather than ask. By asking, I allowed Hayden the opportunity to create the experience surrounding the death of his goldfish—a simple but not always easy child-rearing practice.

Kids: They dance before they learn there is anything that isn't music.

William Stafford

Life's Not Fair

My brother has a fabulous approach when addressing the "it's not fair" conversation with kids. Mike has two lovely girls, five and seven. If and when the complaint arises, he very playfully responds with this statement: "You're right, life's not fair—it never has been and never will be, and whoever told you it is was lying." Parents tend to go to great lengths to keep things fair for their kids—within the family, at school, and in life in general. Though we want it to be fair, the truth is that it's not, and to set our children up with that expectation is comparable to setting them up with the illusions of the prince and the princess living happily ever after. Life may not be fair, but if you shift your attention and get on with it, it can be rather extraordinary regardless.

Life's not fair; get use to it.

Bill Gates

Choice and Accountability

Bottom line: human beings need to experience choice. The absence of choice can leave both little and big people feeling stifled. Offer your child options – be it a meal, clothing, or a sport – this helps the child become adept at making his reality happen, as opposed to feeling as if life is *happening to him*. Now, if little Nate chose soccer and a few weeks into it he decides he prefers hockey, gently remind him his job is to manage the choice he made. Enforcing this choice is a lesson in accountability. This is an age-appropriate principle to be applied within reason. Obviously you're not going to allow a two-year-old to change her bedtime or pick *any* movie out from the video store. You can, however, allow little Logan dress to himself – even if he feels khakis and a purple Diego shirt look smashing with his pirate belt and sneakers. And so what if he insists on wearing his favorite shirt three days in a row. He's exercising choice over his wardrobe and discovering the power to influence his environment in the process.

You can't make positive choices for the rest of your life without an environment
that makes those choices easy, natural, and enjoyable.

Deepak Chopra

Goal Setting for Kids

Goal setting teaches children how to achieve. Age four or five is a great time to initiate goals conversations, and any age can benefit. Introduce the concept and start small, perhaps learning how to tie shoelaces or saving up for a small toy. The goal process instills creative thinking and fosters perseverance. When you introduce goal setting early on, it has children become fluent in getting what they want out of life. It also cultivates success patterns that they can build upon. It provides a powerful context of making things happen when they say so. This is guaranteed to serve them throughout life.

Those who educate children well are more to be honored than they who produce them; for these only gave them life, those the art of living well.

Aristotle

Guide your Children

Many parents attempt to make up for shortcomings in their own childhoods by living vicariously through their children. Let your child choose who they are and what they desire. Even though you always wanted to be a ballerina, play in the NHL or learn piano, offer your child several choices. When she chooses soccer or he picks gymnastics, celebrate your wonderful parenting skills and your child's freedom to explore who *she is*. Congratulate yourself for presenting your child with esteem building choices—after all, you are raising an adult that must learn to trust they know what's best. Choice is a fundamental component of a healthy self-concept. To deny this creates stifled, conflicted children. In the short term, these children are more likely to exhibit behavioral issues and act defiant. In the long run, as grown-ups, it is more probable they'll experience addiction problems, depression and a plethora of issues all stemming from internal conflict that translates into a lack of confidence.

I have found the best way to give advice to your children is to find out what they want and then advise them to do it.

Harry S. Truman

Be Consistent

Many parents make the mistake of saying the same thing repeatedly . They threaten to take some action, but then neglect to follow through. This is ineffective parenting, and trains children to ignore messages from you and others adults. Kids that develop the habit of not listening will invariably carry this throughout life, and just because you love them anyway doesn't mean others will. On top of this, with every request you make you are modelling integrity in keeping your word. If you don't keep your word, it is doubtful they will. Some parents feel they are being mean when they impose boundaries. In reality, consider that being mean is sending your child into the world with the expectation that they can disregard rules in school and in life, free of consequences. This is the difference between short-term discomfort and long-term suffering. Do yourself and your child a favor—ask once. It general only takes a couple of times of losing toy, being cut off from their cell phone or a video game for a few days before they quickly learn what works for everyone. Be a parent that's true to your word.

Our children are counting on us to provide two things: consistency and structure.
Children need parents who say what they mean, mean what they say,
and do what they say they are going to do.

Barbara Coloroso

Let Them Fail

It's one of the most fundamental life lessons. It helps them develop resilience, and gives a firsthand experience of life as a numbers game. Our greatest lessons in life rarely surface without adversity. As a parent, you will have the natural urge to protect your child from disappointment – manage this urge. I'm not saying remove the baby gates so your two-year-old can learn about stairs and gravity. But you can allow your 5th grader to try out for the rep team even if you feel certain he lacks the aptitude to play at that level. You never know what will be born from the experience. The real world involves ups and downs. The key is not to shield children, per se, but rather to teach them how to manage obstacles and identify learnings to apply to future situations. Life is unfair, disappointment is guaranteed. Kids benefit tremendously when they learn how to pick themselves up and try again. A child that is sheltered from challenges can become an adult who falls apart and runs and hides at the first sign of rejection. That's no way to live. Many great things in life come down to trial and error – success is one of them.

Don't ever let someone tell you can't do something son. Not even me...

Christopher Gardner

Encourage Debate

Remember, just because you are older than your child does not necessarily mean that you are wiser (safety omitted) – especially within the context of what's possible for them. Consider: They may see things that you can't. If they disagree with one of your rules, generously allow them the opportunity to present their case. Move away from dictatorship in your household and operate within a democracy. If your 12-year-old is a well-adjusted child and she wants a part time job, maybe she knows what she can handle. Allow her the opportunity to present all the reasons she *is* in fact capable of handling a job, school, and extracurricular activities. Any impressive case should be met with a trial and perhaps an acknowledgment for being creative and standing up with conviction. It's time to give up knowing what's best for our kids. She may in fact be able to maintain her grades while managing all of her current commitments if you simply give her a chance. When you give children permission to WOW you, they often seize the opportunity.

Every word, facial expression, gesture, or action on the part of a parent gives the child some message about self-worth. It is sad that so many parents don't realize what messages they are sending.

Virginia Satir

Trust

The main objective as a parent is to equip your child with tools and a healthy self-concept to live a successful life. Your job is to help them discover who they are – *not* create who they are. Think guidance, not government. Most parents want their children to have an easy life and make choices that result in fulfillment and a happy existence. The fact is, how many parents go about this is counter-productive. They impose their beliefs about what is appropriate for a child or teenager, often resulting in conflict on both ends. The human spirit is very delicate. If and when a child or adolescent shuts down, it can be very difficult to restore this spirit to its natural state. Trust you have equipped your kids with values and tools for life; that you have taught them to think for themselves and stand up when it matters. Exercise faith, and remember that they have an internal compass of who they are becoming in the world. Above all else, get out of their way and become a cheerleader for whatever it is they want! This is powerful parenting, aka Love in Action.

Your kids require you most of all to love them for who they are,
not to spend your whole time trying to correct them.

Bill Ayers

Agreement is not Respect

Many parents want their children to agree with what they believe. Stop that! Unless it involves safety, let them discover and explore their individual viewpoint. They can love you – and you them – while sharing varying views. Children will repress parts of themselves that are not embraced by the Parent Gods. It takes a strong person to allow others their beliefs, without attempting to conform them to agreement – especially in a family environment. Honoring your child's beliefs is no different than respecting your neighbor's choice of car color or religion. You show your child the ultimate reverence and respect when you honor who *she* chooses to be. You are also modeling extraordinary parenting techniques to them that will likely be passed on to your future grandchildren. How's that for a Win–Win!?

Your children are not your children. They are the sons and daughters of Life's longing for itself. They came through you but not from you and though they are with you yet they belong not to you.

Khalil Gibran

Rejuvenation & Play

We must always change, renew, rejuvenate ourselves; otherwise, we harden.

Johann Wolfgang von Goethe

A New Day

When you begin your day tomorrow, try this: Identify several characteristics you can bring to your day, as a way of being that can make a difference in your overall experience. This may be enthusiasm, focus, excitement, gratitude, humor, discipline, or perhaps playfulness. Throughout your day, remind yourself from moment to moment to live from this commitment, regardless of the activity you are performing or the circumstances life presents to you. You can do this at home and at work. At the end of the day, check in and evaluate your progress. You might be surprised at how much you get done, or simply amazed by your ability to experience a new level of fun!

Every person is the creation of himself, the image of his own thinking and believing. As individuals think and believe, so they are.

Claude M. Bristol

Indulge Once in a While

This book is designed to revamp your perspective and improve your life, yes, but if you landed on this page, chances are you could benefit from some indulgence once in a while. Remember, it's not what you do occasionally that shapes your life – it's what you do most of the time. Have a few spoonfuls of decadent cheesecake, purchase that expensive item you've contemplated for months, take a well deserved break and play hooky for an afternoon – have another glass of wine if you'll enjoy it. On the path of self-improvement, many swing the pendulum so far the other way that discipline and sacrifice become the sole experience. It's imperative to connect with joy while you manage your commitments to a better life. Live a little, damn it!

Time you enjoy wasting was not wasted.

John Lennon

Laughter

Here's an interesting fact that can have an amusing impression on your life: Have you ever noticed how wonderful it feels to have a big belly laugh? Perhaps you've giggled so much your belly felt as if you'd just finished a thousand sit-ups, or maybe you reached the point where you were in hysterics for so long your face hurt from smiling. When we laugh, our hypothalamus and pituitary gland release endorphins. Endorphins resemble opiates in their ability to provide pain relief to the body. They also create a sense of calm and over-all well-being. I know - you may be thinking, "That's nice, but how often do I have a really good laugh like that?" What's fabulous about this is that scientists have discovered that regardless of whether the laugh is authentic or not, your body automatically sends out the happy juice. Essentially, pretending to laugh has the same biochemical impact on the body as actual laughter. The funny thing is, when people do this, they often end up laughing at the pretend laugh – generating true laughter. Try it, try it now – I don't mind that you're on a bus or at the office, just go for it!

Laughter is a tranquilizer with no side effects.

Arnold Glasow

Life Mission

Your purpose in life is your mission, and if you're fortunate, you can identify it by looking to your natural talents and passions. What are you drawn too? What are you doing when you lose all track of time? For some of you, your mission is obvious. There's just no denying it, like Barbara Streisand, who was born to sing (she knew this from an early age). For others, your mission can change as you evolve. Actress Jessica Alba started The Honest Co., after having a child and finding it difficult to find baby safe merchandise. Her company promotes eco-friendly, high quality non-toxic products for infants. Your purpose may be born of a challenge, as with Michael J. Fox, who was diagnosed with Parkinson's disease in 1991. He has since gone on to start a foundation and campaign for stem-cell research for healing. He credits the disease with helping him become a better father and husband. Some uncover their life's purpose at age five —others at age fifty-five. By getting active in your community, saying "yes" to invitations, and dabbling with your passions, your life mission will inevitably disclose itself to you, it may have already!

Here's the test to find whether your mission on Earth is finished: if you're alive, it isn't.

Richard Bach

Be a Yes to Life!

Most of the wonderful outcomes that have occurred in your life involve getting off the couch and out into the world. In fact, I bet your greatest accomplishments were initiated through brave actions. Nearly everything worth experiencing on this beautiful planet involves perceived risk, or requires you to challenge your comfort zone: a new job; a first date; classes at the university; or simply dining out with a new group of friends. In all likelihood, you won't find your dream life or attract a new opportunity in the comfort of your living room, watching re-runs of *Friends*. True or true? See, people are either a *Yes* or a *No* to life. My niece Erin, for example, is a Yes to life. I could literally invite her to a hypo-allergenic Poodle Race and she'd jump at the occasion for a new experience. I know Erin's up for anything. As a result, she tends to attract many incredible people and opportunities. Cindy, on the other hand, is a *No* to life. She regularly turns down invitations and shies away from anything new. Erin's world expands while Cindy's world shrinks. It takes only one word to invite new people and adventures into your life, and that word is Yes!

The best things that have ever happened to you in life, happened because you said yes to something. Otherwise things just sort of stay the same.

Danny Wallace – Yes Man

The Simple Pleasures List

Compile a list of all of the Simple Pleasures that make you happy and be sure to sprinkle a few of them throughout your day. Your list may look something like this:

1. Enjoying the pastel sunrise and a cup of tea.
2. Juicing fresh fruits and vegetables.
3. Looking at properties for sale in Europe.
4. Writing an inspiring article.
5. A bucket of balls at the driving range.
6. Surfing resorts online for my next trip.
7. A cappuccino en route to the market.
8. An hour at the go-cart track with my nephews.
9. Fresh lavender from the garden in my bath.
10. The smell of burning wood coming from my fireplace.

You may find that pleasure arrives from simply writing out your List of Pleasures.

Think big thoughts but relish small pleasures.

H. Jackson Brown

Personal Development Programs

The first personal development program I did was a three-day intensive in the year 2000. At the time, I read a lot of growth-based psychology books. I still do. Back then, I was the first person to offer advice to the people around me. I was perplexed and impressed when others were able to apply the information in what appeared to be an effortless transformation. Personally, I could recite information but had little experience with application. After registering for my first course, I remember feeling reluctant and scared. Though I couldn't identify exactly what had me so unsettled then, I can now. At the time, I was so busy pretending to be happy and showing people I had a good life – that I had it all together – that I couldn't see the truth myself. The reality of the situation was that I didn't have it all together – in fact, I didn't know how to be happy. I only knew how to act happy, and the "act as if" wasn't working for me. That three-day investment was life altering. Though I recommend one annually, allocate at least one weekend of your life to a Personal Development Program.

Let us strive to improve ourselves, for we cannot remain stationary;
one either progresses or retrogrades.

Mme. Du Deffand

Take the Leap!

A terrific way to experience change is to be drastic –thoughtful and drastic, that is. It's common for people to over-think their options before acting. Some of you have been contemplating taking action for years, ruminating on the what-ifs. Time to stop contemplating and act! This moment IS the access to better, more interesting moments in the future. What you choose to do with now creates your future. You design it by the way you choose to spend your time and precious thought energy at this very moment. The choice to eat well today will be seen as a result well in the future. A commitment to save could show up as a wonderful European vacation down the road. Choosing to register for a course and begin your studies might translate into a degree or even a pilot's license a few years out. Action keeps you engaged in the moment and looking forward to the future. Stop agonizing over making the "right" choice and simply make A choice. If there's a decision you've been contemplating for some time, or if you're simply inspired to design a series of exciting tomorrows, take the leap and initiate the first steps today, now, this very moment! GO!

Leap and the net will appear!

John Borroughs

Rejuvenate

North America operates under a go–go–go result oriented philosophy. This is especially true of Corporate North America. For many of you, by the end of the day you're completely spent, barely able to stay awake for the journey home. Caffeine–infused energy drinks, coffee, and colas are what prevent you from falling asleep on the return commute. The last thing you want to do is exercise, keep your dinner commitment, or use the tickets to the play you've been looking forward to all year long – but this is exactly the time when you need it the most. Your world shrinks when you become stuck in one train of thought for too long. Shift gears and muster up that morsel of energy to connect with a fresh environment and explore various means to recharge. Sometimes the last thing you feel like doing is exactly what is prescribed to reignite your perspective and restore internal vitality.

Our mental and emotional diets determine our overall energy levels, health and well-being more than we realize. Every thought and feeling no matter how big or small, impacts our inner energy reserves.

Doc Childre

A Busy Mind is a Happy Mind

Keep yourself occupied with projects that inspire you. Purpose is what propels us out of bed each morning, putting the effervescent ZAP back in the eternal gap. Every single one of us needs a mission. Whether it's raising happy healthy children and being a role model as a parent or building a holistic company that brings balance to the world, purpose is the main ingredient for overall well-being. Train yourself to consistently shift your attention to things worthy of your life energy, be it contributing to the people in your life and community or simply puttering around the garden. Joy and peace favor an active mental state – so get movin'!

Pleasure and action make the hours seem short.

William Shakespeare

Find Ways to Restore Your Zen

One of my special things to do in order to gain perspective and restore my Zen is to visit Starbucks at varying locations. I love the intrigue that different spaces bring. Upon entering, I scope out the most comfy chair I can see, usually near a window. I curl up with a cup of Java or a Zen Green Tea. Sometimes I read a magazine or write – occasionally I just watch the world, people coming and going, popping in for one of life's simple pleasures. It's the perfect sanctuary, a mental retreat that helps me reconnect to inspiration. Life can be that simple. A few deep breaths, a cup of Java, a cozy chair, and voila – my Zen perspective is restored.

Starbucks represents something beyond a cup of coffee.

Howard Schultz

Relationships

We're born alone, we live alone, we die alone. Only through our love and friendship can we create the illusion for the moment that we're not alone.

Orson Welles

Love as an Action

Easy peasy, this one's simple. When you truly care about someone, you think about what's important to them, what will affect them, and act accordingly. You choose to operate from a long-term consequence model. Consider the fact that the truest expression of love is when another person's desires and wants supersede your own. This means that everything you do is influenced by considering how they may be impacted by any choices you make, including the people and situations you invite into your life.

True love is when someone else's needs trump your own.

Brad Pitt

Enlightenment

If you'd like to evaluate your level of enlightenment, move in with your parents or your adult child for a few weeks. For some of you, a weekend is sufficient time spent to rapidly activate all the patterns you may have thought were long gone and buried. That's right, you'll quickly learn you have plenty of areas yet to be transformed if you're willing to take them on. Really, your family members are a terrific means for highlighting the under-developed parts of your personality – areas where you still have room to grow. The trick is to recognize this as the reminder arrives and then, like a Zen monkey, graciously seize the opportunity!

Why is it that family can always find our buttons?
...Because they installed them!

Unknown

Emotional Fitness

Children unconsciously model behaviors and emotions from the Parent Gods, so what you say has very little impact compared to what you do. If you're truly committed to rearing happy, balanced, wise children, it's essential that you look closely to examine what you are modeling for your children on a daily basis. Take this opportunity to answer a few simple questions: What are you teaching your children about how to manage stress effectively? Do you address problems head on? Are you presenting an example of emotional fitness for your family? Have you found ways to communicate respectfully with the people around you? Are you able to hear other people's points of view and respond in a gracious manner? What messages are you sending about nutrition? What about integrity and managing promises? Use your children as your very own little Zen Masters to gauge when you are modeling life situations in a healthy and effective manner. Consciously sculpt a growth-based blueprint of a well rounded, exemplary individual that brings harmony and balance to your own existence so your children have a solid reference to model.

Setting an example is not the main means of influencing another, it's the only means.

Albert Einstein

Breakups

These can be tough, with both parties left feeling unappreciated, confused, and even unlovable. A breakup tends to surface insecurities and trigger dormant emotions – this is why the breakdown of a relationship can leave you feeling as if you've been hit by a bus! When having this experience, it's perfectly normal to want to find fault with the other person, but that won't help you – being accountable will. It's like this: When you remove blame you reconnect with power. Even if your former partner or spouse did lie, mislead you, or cheat, to restore power you must find it in yourself to be responsible for the fact that you picked that person. You may have even had a few clues that things could go this way and chose to ignore them. If you're willing to explore what you overlooked because some characteristics were exactly what you wanted, you can become responsible for the outcome. Take ownership – when you accept cause in the matter, it allows you to look forward and design a future. Every ending is a new beginning, so be conscious when you choose your ending, as it has the power to influence your next beginning.

When we are in love, we are convinced nobody else will do. But as time goes, others do do, and often do do, much much better.

Coco J. Ginger

A Stable Self-Concept

If you're skinny and someone tells you you're fat, you may look at the person and wonder if perhaps their vision is impaired. When people make comments that you're certain are untrue, it's easy to roll your eyes and instantly let it go. See, it's not what someone says to you that matters – it's what you say about what they said, that has the power. If a person points out that you've let yourself go and you're looking worn and exhausted, chances are you're already aware and may say something to yourself such as, "Well, I guess I can't hide it. Everyone knows I'm stressed." The upset is caused by what you said, not what they said. Since there's rarely any value in blaming; give up resisting others' opinions, forego the auto-reaction. Get working on whatever will make you feel better and ultimately support your overall vision.

As long as a man stands in his own way, everything seems to be in his way.

Ralph Waldo Emerson

Marriage Versus the Expensive Party

The average bride will easily spend 300 hours planning her wedding. Guess how many hours the average couple actually spends planning their marriage? That's right – on average, I would say less than five hours. People put tens of thousands of dollars and hundreds of hours into planning a one-day event, and then more than 70% end up divorcing. Can you imagine starting a business by this model? Imagine saying to someone, "Yes, I am going to have a big launch party for my business, spend a small fortune – 10,000–50,000 dollars. It will be a great party! Yet I have no business plan, no long-term vision for the company. I'm not sure if there is a market for the product, but hey, I'll just wing it and see." For that business to work out it would require a lot of luck! Yet we have the audacity to expect success in marriage after planning a party. If you really want a marriage – and most don't – begin by addressing the fundamentals, like religion, child rearing, scheduling holiday's with two families, finances, values alignment and communication. Doing so will give your marriage a chance. Divorce is painful– even when correcting a poor choice.

Love does not consist of gazing at each other but in looking in the same direction.

Antoine de Saint-Exupery

Take a Deep Breath – Then Communicate

Human beings receive messages based on the dominant emotion within the communication, not necessarily the words or information you're intending to relay. A raised voice implies disapproval and anger, even if it's raised due to safety or concern. Talking to someone from a state of agitation will pass along frustration that can be easily interpreted as condemnation. Momentarily step away from any charged situation and diffuse heightened emotion by visiting your mental sanctuary. When you return to the conversation, know that your message will be best received when you express yourself in a calm tone and from a relaxed perspective. Exercise awareness and become conscious of the emotion behind your words, particularly when having delicate conversations that impact important areas of life. It's simple – conversations shift when you shift and choose to focus on the solution.

The older I grow the more I listen to people who don't talk much.

Germain G. Glien

Falling in Love

So you met a beautiful soul and fell in love. Have you ever considered who it is you actually fell in love with? When people split up, the general complaint is "you're not the person I fell in love with." Consider this: The person you fell in love with was you, and the feelings you had in the presence of that person at that date and time. Yippy for that! How utterly fantastic – if you have or do split, you still get to be with you!

When you like who you are alone with you are never alone.

Wayne Dyer

Address the Issue

Dana and John were contemplating breaking up, but they had two kids together. Reminiscing on what went well in their relationships, they realized they were always very much a team when they were expecting and taking care of a newborn. They decided if they had another baby, it just might help them rekindle their connection and stay together. It did divert them for a while, but ultimately their problems and frustrations were only amplified by their growing family. This is far too common. If you feel you and your partner are growing in different directions, a child may distract you from that temporarily, but it doesn't address the issue. Don't have a child when you want your relationship to last – have a therapist instead, who will likely tell you that under no circumstances will having an additional child alleviate your relationship issues.

Almost no one is foolish enough to imagine that he automatically deserves great success in any field of activity; yet almost everyone believes that he automatically deserves success in marriage.

Sydney J. Harris

The Naked Argument

Next time you have an argument with your partner (provided you're in a suitable environment), strip down and continue on with the disagreement in your birthday suit. It's very difficult to remain angry and ignore opportunities for solutions when you're naked. Couples tend to be more open, resolute, and playful when discussing serious issues in the buff. If you're honestly committed to a breakthrough, there are many creative ways to shift the tone of a conversation with your sweetheart. This is one of my favorites!

> *Humor results when society says you can't scratch certain things in public, but they itch in public.*
>
> *Tom Walsh*

Love 'Em Anyway

When people close to you get on your nerves – and if you're breathing, they will – ask yourself this question: "Can I love them anyway?" It tends to put things into perspective. No matter how enlightened you think you are, occasionally there will be qualities in your family members, mate, and close acquaintances you find difficult to embrace. By asking yourself this very important question, you potentially diffuse your reaction and presence yourself to the love you have for the individual, independent of idiosyncrasies or varying viewpoints. Remember, people will show up exponentially based on your focal point at any given time. When you choose to love them anyway, it puts you in charge of the focus and invites warm fuzzies into the equation.

I would rather be able to appreciate things I cannot have than to have things I am not able to appreciate.

Elbert Hubbard

The Fairy Tale Myth

By now, many of you have discovered the Fairy Tale myth. Relationships don't generally deliver on the illusive "happily ever after" concept, and it is not realistic to make one person responsible for your happiness – unless of course that person is you! In childhood we are heavily conditioned with beliefs about the world by the well-intentioned Parent Gods. Come preschool, most little girls are enamored with tales of the prince and princess living happily ever after. The truth is, relationships are much like life: they're filled with ups and downs and subject to ever-changing dynamics. Some days they're amazing and others days they present an unwelcome level of frustration. Give up the view that it should be any other way than it is. When you approach every partnership challenge with non-resistance, it becomes a learning tool to grow and fulfill on the bigger picture. If you choose to surrender to your differences, you may find your partner is precisely who you need to help develop a very important part of yourself. Every experience has value – often more so than credit is assigned.

I will love the light for it shows me the way, yet I will endure
the darkness because it shows me the stars.

Og Mandino

Looking for Evidence

Do you remember when you first met that special someone? Bliss was present almost every moment you were together. When apart, you'd catch yourself smiling at the very thought of your new love. During the early stages of love it's natural to magnify virtues and overlook foibles. In fact, in the beginning almost everything they do or say reinforces how utterly perfect they are for you. You looked for evidence of perfection and you found it. Fast forward a few years and chances are you are more present to your partner's annoying quirks than the once long list of compelling compatibility factors. Admit it, perfect is the last adjective you'd use to describe your mate. Provided your values are aligned, the relationship was likely a sound choice and will continue to be. Begin the process of looking at your partner with new eyes and presence yourself to all the qualities that supported your initial choice. Or, you could find someone new and start over – but be advised, when you leave in a state of blame it is common to gravitate to a individual with personality characteristics that are very similar to the ones in your current mate.

Sometimes it is the person closest to us who must
travel the furthest distance to be our friend.

Robert Brault

Stop It!

I conceive that pleasures are to be avoided if greater pains be the consequence, and pains to be coveted that will terminate in greater pleasures.

Michel De Montaigne

Justification

Justification is the practice of inventing an excuse to do something that you're conflicted about or that violates your value system. Humans can justify anything – but at what cost? "I'll just have one more dessert and start my healthy lifestyle tomorrow." The price: self-loathing. "Eventually I'll earn enough money to pay for everything I am putting on my credit card." Yet it consumes you. "It's only sex ." Still you question if you deserve the one you're with. "It's all her fault, I had nothing to do with it." Yet it keeps you up at night. "He's cruel, he deserves this!" But it hurts more than just him. Justifying is easy to do, especially if you're clever. People justify cheating, obesity, addictions, lying, stealing, racism, and hate. Bottom line: Justifying generates guilt and further issues. Broaden your choice clarity and live free from the habit of justifying actions that you know are detrimental to you and others. Two questions to ask yourself when initiating a questionable course of action: "Is this coming from love?" and, "Could I feel peaceful about this choice if the world was watching?" Always remember – the world is watching through you.

Thought is the sculpture who creates who you want to be.

Henry David Thoreau

Ruminating

We have all had devastating experiences. A friend or loved one dies unexpectedly. Someone promised to be there for you and disappeared in moments of crisis, when you needed them most. Opportunities that would have made your life better had they only played out like they were meant to. If only... When something unfair happens or someone wrongs you, some of you will relive that unfavorable memory, allowing it to take over to the point where it consumes you. Thoughts that are intensely ruminated on powerfully imprint themselves on the psyche and eventually become part of your identity. The issue then becomes *how* you think about what happened, *not* what happened. So what's worse? The moment you experienced when you lost something or someone – or the fact that you have chosen to relive the sadness in your mind every day since? A person or unexpected event can impact you once, but ruminating on it can impact you forever.

The great art of life is sensation, to feel that we exist, even in pain.

Lord Byron

Are You Should-ing on People?

Human beings have what I call "Rules for Unhappiness" – expectations of others that show up as "shoulds." These pesky little rules are invisible and can derail our connection with the present moment, sending some into a tizzy in a matter of seconds. For example: Others *should* say thank you. My boss *should* address me in a respectful tone. How about this one? Customer service reps *should* be pleasant and know that as a customer I am always right! Though you may in fact agree, the above-mentioned "shoulds" are a recipe for dissatisfaction. On a daily basis, I guarantee you will run into all sorts of people who think differently than you and in turn disagree with your rules. Inadvertently, they will test your commitment to happiness and challenge your ability to let go. Some you may interpret to be rude, or thoughtless. The truth is, you never know what people may be dealing with in their lives when they snap, cut you off or behave with seeming disregard. Next time you bump up against a discrepancy of rules, challenge yourself to maintain a positive perspective regardless of how you believe others *should* behave.

What we see depends mainly on what we look for.

John Lubbock

People Pleasers

People pleasers appease those in their environment to get approval. They forgo their own happiness in the hopes of being liked. People pleasers generate a certain codependency by morphing into a chameleon to avoid conflict at all cost. Externally there appears to be harmony, but internally, being a people pleaser comes with a hefty price: often resenting the person you're placating, silently lamenting over what you really want to say or do. Ultimately, when you live for the endorsement of your environment, you train others with the expectation that you will always agree with them. Sadly, this process erodes self-confidence. People tend to develop this way of being from a dominant Parent God that collapsed love and agreement. "Do it my way and I'll love you – do it your way and I'll remove love." It's born out of survival and maintained through habit. Interested in a remedy? Gently begin to express your truth in a manner that's kind and non-threatening. Catch yourself and tell the truth: "I just agreed with you to keep the harmony, but the fact is that I have a different opinion." Then, congratulate yourself for expressing your truth.

We are so accustomed to disguise ourselves to others that in
the end we become disguised to ourselves.

François Duc de La Rochefoucauld

Perfectionist

Nothing immobilizes people like attempting perfection. It can derail creativity, eradicate pleasure, and interfere with appreciating life's current treasures. Perfectionists are rarely satisfied. People with this trait are likely to notice and get stuck on miniscule mistakes and are momentarily incapable of seeing beyond them. For example, a perfectionist may receive an inspiring letter of acknowledgement from someone they care for deeply. But if the letter contains a spelling error, they may bypass the entire message of love, wondering how someone could possibly be so careless. Being intensely critical with unrealistic expectations robs people of their life source and connection with others. If you happen to recognize yourself on this page, you can take steps to disengage the habit. Like any new way of being, it takes training. So try this: For every flaw you see in yourself or the people and things around you, start to balance this awareness by recognizing three positives within the situation. Tune into your internal dialogue and begin to generate conversations of acceptance and flexibility. Focus on appreciating all the people and riches in your life, here, right now.

Does "anal-retentive" have a hyphen?

Alison Bechdel

Sympathy

Sometimes when we complain we receive sympathy from those in our midst. Occasionally this is fine, but be cautious with sympathy, as it can unknowingly become a tool for attention. For some, ailments become fused with one's identity surfacing in every conversation. Grumbling about aches and pains directs your awareness to them and is liable to magnify the condition – be it a blister, a toothache, or a more serious ailment. If you experience ongoing discomfort, try shifting your focus to health. Experiment with different types of healing remedies just to see what happens. Get busy with feel good choices such as exercises classes, nutritional awareness, or an acupuncture treatment. There is also the option of remote healing, reflexology, and Chinese herbal medicine. Anything you focus your attention on expands, so be responsible to assure that which garners your attention is indeed expansion worthy.

There is something terribly morbid in the modern sympathy with pain.
One should sympathize with the color, the beauty, the joy of life.
The less said about life's sores the better.

Oscar Wilde

Take a Holiday from Victimville

We've all had a chance to visit Victimville at one time or another. It's no fun at all. Victimville is a perspective you visit when you become prey to a life choice, a person, or, said another way, your own thinking. Try this, regardless of whether you love it or not – adopt the philosophy that everything currently in your life you somehow attracted as a learning tool. Yes, everything – including that bad investment, nasty boss, or selfish person with a frozen heart that you keep forgiving, knowing they'll likely never behave any other way. Give up the attitude of "I am this way because of what happened to me in the past." You are this way because you think how you do at this moment. Enough already! Take power over YOU. Bottom line: When you blame, you surrender your power to external forces. Learn to interrupt this inclination. Recognize when you're on the road to Victimville and quickly re-course!

> *If it's never our fault, we can't take responsibility for it. If we can't take responsibility for it, we'll always be its victim.*
>
> *Richard Bach*

The Obesity Epidemic

I'm curious. Isn't telling a grossly obese person to "love your size" the same as encouraging an alcoholic or heroin addict to love their addiction even though it may likely kill them? From what I understand, obesity related deaths match those of alcoholism and tobacco use. Perhaps it's time to stop pretending that food addictions are beyond our control or somehow exempt from the addiction category. They too do damage through self-humiliation, shame the children face by being teased for their own weight issues, or the embarrassment that comes with being picked up from school by a very large parent. All addictions relate to a poor decision making process in coping skills. It's a choice to deal with problems by means of numbing or creating a temporary high, as is gambling, shopping, and many other types of addiction. At some point, the user's behavior becomes habitually unconscious, creating the illusion that there is no choice in the behavior. The individual likely designs an identity around the addiction. It may not feel like it, but it is indeed still a choice. As long as it's a choice, people can envision another choice – if they so choose.

When addicts withdraw from the substances of addiction, feelings surface.

Kay Sheppard

211

Jekyll & Hyde Commitment

Is your foot on the brake in life, or the gas pedal? Perhaps you're one of those who keeps their foot on the gas and the brake simultaneously. You engage in three days of exercise and healthy eating, only to find yourself bingeing again. In the event you're living the Jekyll and Hyde approach to your goals, what's likely absent is a clearly imprinted vision of you acting out the new way of being, ultimately as a lifestyle or habit. It's important to presence yourself to exactly why you chose that goal. If you're operating from the Jekyll and Hyde tactic and it's new, it can represent progress, the transition of awareness, and adjustment as you integrate new patterns. If this is the case, be sure to celebrate any growth. Now, if you have been doing it for several years, it's more likely a self-sabotage tactic stemming from an unconscious duality of self. Either way, the remedy is patience, choice, and a continued reinforced picture of your vision on the deepest level possible.

You are not here merely to make a living. You are here in order to enable the world to
live more amply, with greater vision, with a finer spirit of hope and achievement.
You are here to enrich the world, and you impoverish
yourself if you forget the errand.

Woodrow Wilson

The Design of Guilt

Guilt can teach us to exercise choice reflective of our value systems. Its design is to educate in order to execute change. As a default emotion, guilt is one of the most barren mental states one can visit or attempt to create in another individual. If you're trying to make someone else feel guilty, you may want to look at what value that really has for you. Is it the illusion of building yourself up, being superior? Putting the other person down as an attempt to dominate? It may be that allowing someone to control you with this emotion gets you off the hook for making powerful life choices. If you're in a relationship that functions on the foundation of guilt – either frequent feelings of guilt for not measuring up or doing your best to leave someone else feeling guilty – visit the purpose of living a life entangled in this bleak emotion. You may be mimicking transactions from the Parent Gods, and doing so is not conducive to emotional freedom or happiness for either party involved. Learn to engage healthy emotional frequencies that support well-being not just for you, but those around you too.

Guilt should be a momentary pang to spur one into corrective action.
Anything longer is wasted, and worse, selfish.

Mark Belletini

Awareness Hell

Over the past decade I've witnessed some brilliant information on change go mainstream. Movies such as *The Secret* and *What the Bleep Do We Know* have made their way into video stores, making transformational tools accessible to everyone. Though awareness is the first step on the path to change, discerning in the absence of action can create the ultimate convolution. Awareness Hell is the process of witnessing a pattern within yourself, engaging in self-loathing because of it, and doing nothing proactive to transform the state. It's a type of self-sabotage, and its origin is the same as what created the issues to begin with. Self-awareness is not designed to turn you into the Thought Nazi by being used as a reprimand tool – and don't belittle yourself for doing so, either, because it happens to the best of us. Remember, most everything you have become to date was produced gradually – and that, my friend, is precisely how it will change. Get busy implementing structures to support the new you. Today, identify one tiny action you can take – a new approach from previous attempts that'll initiate a direction worthy of celebration.

Just because everything is different doesn't mean anything has changed.

Irene Peter

Tools, Distinctions, & Resources

I've found that luck is quite predictable.
If you want more luck, take more chances.
Be more active. Show up more often.

Brian Tracy

215

Affirmations

If you really want to expedite life results, affirmations are an incredible tool. They do work. Here's what you need to know about affirmations to ensure efficacy: All affirmations must have an action and a feeling word – it's what motivates the brain to act. Generally speaking, you can repeat your affirmation 20–100 times and see nothing. When you approach 1,000, 5,000, or 20,000 repetitions, you'll notice your actions and behaviors beginning to align with your ultimate outcome. Sound like a lot of work? That's the resignation in you talking. You're having approximately 60,000–70,000 thoughts per day as it is, and affirmations ensure that they work in your favor. Train yourself to passionately repeat a power statement: "I am happily and easily earning $15,000.00 per month or more" or "I am prepared, early, and on time for all meetings." Gradually your unconscious mind will begin to accept the message you're feeding it as truth, and inevitably fire ideas and thoughts to help you build exactly that. You see, you're having thoughts anyway – why not imprint your mind to have them support you to create what you want?

Any idea, plan, or purpose may be placed in the mind through repetition of thought.

Napoleon Hill

Positive Expression

The English language consists of approximately half a million words. Of those half a million, there are just over 3,000 to articulate emotions. Two thirds of those 3,000 words express negative emotions, leaving somewhere around 1,000 words for happiness and positive expression. It's no wonder people find it effortless to take a defeatist perspective. By mere volume our language is set up to easily articulate that which is not working in life. Understand that your choice of words influences how you feel about a situation, and subsequently have the capacity to shape an outcome. Knowing that words also carry an emotional charge, be conscious to choose words that add levity to an experience. Next time you find yourself feeling a little down, why not label your mood as "disenchanted" instead of depressed? Or something unwelcome may be "unfavorable" rather than awful. When you become conscientious of your language, you support yourself to better align with that which you DO want.

Words mean more than what is set down on paper. It takes the human voice to infuse them with deeper meaning.

Mary Angelou

The Wheel of Life

The Wheel of Life is a tool to identify where you can best put your attention to increase balance. Grade yourself in each area on a scale of 1–10 (10 illustrates fulfillment, with a 1 implying neglect). For the artistic type, you can color the percentage, from 0%–100%. Just like a wheel, the journey will be a little bumpy if a few of the spokes are missing. Personalize the wheel to reflect the top eight areas of your life. You may wish to add Spirituality, Contribution, or something else. Check in with yourself on a monthly basis to observe progress. Visit lifesinsession.ca to download a blank wheel to customize the headings.

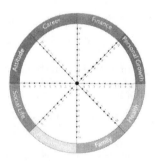

I believe that being successful means having a balance of success stories across the many areas of your life. You can't truly be considered successful in your business life if your home life is in shambles.

Zig Ziglar

20 Actions to a Breakthrough

I have a theory: At any given time we are 20 significant actions away from a breakthrough. If you want a more toned body, think about the difference 20 workouts would make in the re-shaping of your physique over a three- to four-week period. Attending 20 job interviews could provide you with your dream job or a part time income to purchase that timeshare in Hawaii. Your messy house could be organized most certainly with 20 sizable actions. What about green juice for dinner for 20 consecutive days? I bet you'd proudly fit into something that's a bit too tight right now — not to mention you'll restore mental clarity! To intentionally execute a life breakthrough, make a list of 20 actions that can provide you with one!

Dreams pass into the reality of action. From the actions stems the dream again; and this interdependence produces the highest form of living.

Anais Nin

Learning Happy

"My parents don't express positive emotions – it's not in my genes to be happy." If you didn't watch people around you express happiness when your neural patterns (brain patterns) were being formed from a very young age, it may feel unnatural and require effort. Or, you may have been punished or had love taken away by the Parent Gods when expressing joy. Parents utter the craziest things, like, "Stop laughing, stop having fun!" This can create a belief that fun and happiness are not okay. Believe it or not, such messages interpreted as beliefs can impact you even decades later. But no matter how miserable your folks may have been, you're a grown up now – it is safe to feel and express joy. The tone with which you carry yourself through life is now your responsibility – you are the creator of your own happy self and it will take practice if it was not modeled for you. Stick with it – unless, of course, you're happy being unhappy.

The words "I am" are potent words; be careful what you hitch them to. The thing you're claiming has a way of reaching back and claiming you.

A.L. Kitselman

The Language Vernacular

The words we use shape our experience, so be sure to choose wisely. Have your language be concise and tailored to the person or group you're speaking with. For example, if I am delivering a workshop to a wellness center, I may use what I jokingly label woo-woo terms, such as "the law of attraction" and "the universe." That same course delivered in a corporate environment would be packaged specifically to support the listening of the intended audience. I'd engage my corporate vernacular, offering "thinking resources for peak performance," and make statements such as, "quantum physics dictates..." with scientific data and studies to back it up. Although I am presenting the same distinctions, they're designed for each audience and how they interpret certain words and terminology. Using words that people don't identify with or have strong opinions about can shut down their listening very quickly and cause them to miss valuable information – information they would otherwise absorb when presented in their native communication style.

I would never use a long word where a short one would answer the purpose. I know there are surgeons in this country who "ligate" arteries. Other surgeons only tie them, and it stops the bleeding just as well.

Oliver Wendell Holmes

Observe the State of Another

Next time you experience someone in your environment that is angry allow yourself to observe their disposition without judging it. Physically take one step back to separate yourself from their energy field. Then, take a few deep breaths in through the nose and out through the mouth. Many of our emotions feel involuntary – a reflex to stimuli when the nervous system feels threatened. That being said, when confronted, you literally have a matter of seconds to interrupt your amygdale brain and replace the unconscious reactionary synapse that's about to reign. Learn to overcome this chemical process. Exercise the power to allow another to experience their emotions without unconsciously mirroring their mood. When you judge a person's mood you often take on the very energy you wish to escape. It certainly isn't the first reflex, but with practice it is possible to step outside of the trigger and recognize the emotional state without making the individual or situation wrong that it is – how it is. You're then free to respond in a tone YOU set for the conversation.

All things are subject to interpretation. Whichever interpretation prevails at a given time is a function of power and not truth.

Friedrich Nietzsche

The Mirror Exercise

While taking an international course, a group of us were asked to do a self love exercise that initially seemed somewhat odd. The instruction was to stand in front of the mirror and look at yourself and notice what you like about your physical presence. Then state "I love you until you believed it. After thinking, "This will be easy," I looked and quickly looked away. I first noticed my freckles. I recalled in grade three being told it looked like I was standing behind a screen door when s#@! was thrown at me. It hurt to think about that memory. Then I looked at my green eyes that I had always wished were blue. I remembered a boy I liked saying I was so pretty until I removed my sunglasses. Tears streamed down my face as I realized I had used these childhood events as proof I was unattractive, I had no idea. I kept looking...I stared at my button nose and began to be grateful as I let go of my need to find flaws and criticize myself. I started chanting "I Love you" until the "yeah rights" stopped and I began to believe what I was saying. Slowly but surely I witnessed this beautiful green-eyed women emerge, who loved herself, freckles and all.

The question is not what you look at but what you see.

Henry David Thoreau

Heal Your Patterns with Compassion

When you recognize a pattern in yourself, embrace it no matter how unfavorable it may appear. Every pattern you have in your life was designed by you to avoid pain or increase pleasure – whether it was an unconscious creation when you were five or twenty-five, it's a survival mechanism intended to protect you. When you criticize a pattern, it only creates resistance against the desired state, having the pattern come back even stronger. Take a moment to visualize and connect with the vulnerable part of you that created the pattern and the need it fulfilled. Acknowledge your pattern for its intention to ease the situation. Understand the pattern and respect the part of yourself that created it. Say aloud, "you have protected me and for that I am grateful. I appreciate the intention and I have outgrown the need for you, but thank you for always wanting to keep me safe. I am now free to move on." Connect with that part of you that has only ever wanted what's best for you, and know the pattern wants that too.

Habit is habit and not to be flung out of the window by any man,
but coaxed downstairs a step at a time.

Mark Twain

Repetition and Access to Transformation

Scientific research shows that the average person operates on an unconscious level approximately 90% of the time. That is, replaying the same behaviors and choices everyday over and over again, regardless of whether the behaviors are creating favorable outcomes or not. In order to create new results, one must choose a new action repeatedly until it becomes unconscious. This involves overpowering the part of you that says it wants to engage the old behavior. Because routine contributes to unconsciousness, changing habitual activities offers direct and timely access to transformation. It could be as simple as taking a new route to work, drinking your coffee black, or trying an exercise class for the first time. To do this, you will need to give up your story about what you like or don't like, or the commonly held belief that change is difficult. The truth is, you can get used to just about anything. When you forego the urge to engage an old neural pattern, you automatically ease the process of change, allowing conscious choice into your life. Keep in mind that the magic ingredient is repetition.

We are what we repeatedly do. Excellence is not an act but a habit.

Aristotle

Euphemism

Euphemism: "The act or an example of substituting a mild, indirect, or vague term for one considered harsh, blunt, or offensive." The perfect example of this is what's said during the safety instructions on an aircraft, when they offer directions in the event of a water landing. What they really mean is "crash", but the word "crash" plants a seed that triggers panic. Apply this principle to your daily life: "I can't stand my partner" could be said another way – "my partner and I are going through an unflattering period." Likewise, 'life feels hopeless" may be stated, "I'm finding it challenging to connect with inspiration." If you repeat, "I'm broke", how do you think that will impact your financial life? The words we choose create emotions and subsequently enhance or detract from an experience. What you say to yourself about an experience becomes the experience. By choosing lighter terms, it is possible to diffuse emotions and eventually shift your perspective from how you may originally interpret a person, or situation. Words create worlds. Change your vocabulary as an experiment to lighten up your life – see how you love it!

Think twice before you speak, because your words and influence will plant the seed of either success or failure in the mind of another.

Napoleon Hill

The Emotional Hangover

An emotional hangover is similar to post traumatic stress disorder. Emotional experiences can get stuck in the cells of the body and can wreak havoc on your well-being. According to Chinese medicine and a published Harvard study (1996), this is how disease is created. Too much energy (yang) or not enough energy (yin) flow to particular areas; subsequently, cells begin to behave unnaturally and complications arise. After a highly stressful emotional experience, take therapeutic action to get your body back in balance. Write your feelings down, Google acupressure home remedies, go for a massage, reflexology, or therapeutic treatment. There are so many amazing cathartic techniques available if you're truly committed to healing. Visit YouTube and experiment with Emotional Freedom Technique (EFT), and discover new ways to clear residual emotions from the body on a cellular level. Your body will thank you for it.

Be sincere in your efforts and appreciate the progress you make, not expecting to be free from unpleasant emotions all at once. It gets easier as you go. When long-standing emotional issues lose some of their intensity and importance, things won't bother you as much.

Doc Childre and Howard Martin

Speak to the Soul

Here's an unconventional communication method that is especially valuable when interacting with heightened emotions, as well as with other various barriers. Think of someone you'd like to positively impact. Imagine a sanctuary in your mind's eye with you sitting across from the individual. Presence yourself to the love and affinity you have for this person. Now, tune into the deep desire behind the intention of the interaction you're about to have. Once you've done this, you're free to ask questions to better understand their position – or it could be you'd like to make a request of the person you're meeting with. A few simple rules while hosting a guest in your mental sanctuary: make sure all interactions are coming from your highest awareness, and do not physically touch the person during this visual interaction. It may be necessary to schedule a few encounters before your message is clearly sent or theirs is received. Have faith. This is the process of bypassing a person's body – where their resistance patterns are stored – to acquire direct access to their spirit.

Everyone is born with psychic abilities. It's just a matter of knowing how to tap into them.

Julien Offray de La Mettrie

Time Management

Not managing your time and making excuses are bad habits. Don't put them together by claiming "I don't have time".

Bo Bennett

Take Three

You'll feel best about yourself and move closer to your vision when you actively employ a task-based accomplishment philosophy. Write a list of three tasks that will move you forward in some area of life. They may be three little chores that provide the sensation that life's taken care of, or the first step of many that bring you closer to a long-term vision. You are guaranteed to experience an elevated sense of pride and purpose when you incorporate the Take Three structure as a daily routine. People thrive on progress. Be it organizational systems to better manage your household or committing to an MBA, getting things done makes us feel good. The reason for this is that human beings consciously and unconsciously assign meaning to absolutely everything. "I exercised so I am proud, I ate junk food all week therefore I am a lazy blob." At any moment you are either moving towards or away from the life you really want. By implementing the Take Three daily structure at the end of each day you can proudly acknowledge you have successfully moved forward.

In life, you're either moving forward or backwards, towards something or away from it, growing stronger or becoming weaker.

Michael Irwin

Mental Junk Food

If you're serious about minimizing your procrastination habit, you will need to manage the plethora of online distractions. Too many of you spend hours on Facebook reading about the strangers you call friends. Each morning you swear today's the day you're going to be super productive, but moments later you find yourself unconsciously logging in. Sound familiar? Or perhaps you're a chronic Texter, Sexter, or Twitterist. You may be someone who spends hours surfing the Internet, being moderately entertained on tabloid websites. Three hours later you wonder where the time went. It's very easy to do. Technology has its advantages, and it has also become an errant time stealer. Watch these habits as they become unconscious quickly– borrowing time that could be better spent forwarding your life and addressing your Bucket List. If your computer had a time reader to gauge your monthly entertainment, I suspect you'd feel there were more resourceful activities of which you could direct your attention. Why not save it for the treadmill or the take a ten minute Internet break? Be wise with your time, knowing that once it's spent, it cannot be recovered.

It's not enough to be busy, so are the ants. The question is, what are we busy about?

Henry David Thoreau

A Prisoner to Things

Over the years, Liz had accumulated many possessions. This was easy for her, given at one point she owned four houses. Eventually, Liz trimmed down to two houses – yet she held onto many of the extras that were once scattered across several properties. Being raised during the depression, she employed the mindset that one should keep things, just in case. She had bins full of kitchen supplies, tools, and linens – enough duplicates to open a bed & breakfast without having to purchase a thing. She spent a lot of time trying to find things and moving stuff about. Her ongoing focus was to organize all the items that may come in handy – one day. She'd become a hostage to clutter. One day, Liz declined a lunch date, using the familiar excuse that she was getting organized. Innocently, her friend inquired when she might be finished, prompting an epiphany. "Never!" she replied, laughing. She hung up the phone and called the Re-use Center for pick-up. In that moment, Liz recognized the absurdity of her behavior and experienced a sense of freedom that had been absent for years.

Present Me is tired of holding onto Future Me's crap.
Future Me will just have to deal with it.

Unknown

Conscious Television

How fortunate we are to have a multitude of programs streamed into our living room offering endless entertainment options. Though modern technology presents several benefits, it also come with a down side. According to AC Neilson, the average person watches 28 hours per week. That's the equivalent of two months per year of uninterrupted television. Even more startling: The average number of 30-second commercials seen in a year by a child is approximately 16,000. There's no surprise it's called "programming" – the programs are bait to capture an audience for the advertisers. Be selective when you choose to watch television. Don't be one of those people that watches show after show, being moderately entertained. I promise you, when you are at the end of your life on your deathbed, you will not feel it was time well spent. Schedule activities in your life that are worthy of your time. There's a world of endless invigorating possibilities available to those that don't allow couching to dominate their lives.

I think it's brought the world a lot closer together, and will continue to do that. There are downsides to everything; there are unintended consequences to everything. The most corrosive piece of technology that I've ever seen is called television, but then again, at its best, is magnificent.

Steve Jobs

Gift Someone Your Undivided Attention

We are wired for sound in the 21st century and can communicate in an instant – it's rather remarkable, really. There's no question this is the information era. Hearing people on their cell phones in a bathroom, sometimes I wonder if we've taken things a bit too far. Do you think Alexander Graham Bell might agree? How about you? When your phone rings, do you sigh and race off to answer it as if you're the President approving some nuclear go ahead? Granted, there are times when you do need to be on call 24/7 – but most of us can give up the idea that every email, text, or call is urgent and should take precedence over the person directly in front of us. Some people use technology to avoid intimacy and create separation. Stop that! Leave a message on voicemail telling callers you'll be retuning calls during a specific time period. Turn off the ringer on your phone and gift your undivided attention to the important person or project that's currently in front of you right now.

Action expresses priorities.

Mahatma Gandhi

Unfinished Business

What have you been meaning to do? Most of us have a long mental list of tasks to complete. Call a friend, thank someone for their help, send photos to relatives, update the books, or complete a project. Allow this book to make a difference for you today. Transfer your list of unfinished business onto a piece of paper. Next to each task, write down the time required to complete it. Now knock off at least one task, starting with the smallest. Do it now. If need be, break the task into small achievable steps, ideally doable in 30 minutes or less. Why is this so important? Each time you think of the unfinished task you'll sigh, feel defeated, and your Internal Broadcaster will reiterate some version of negative self-talk. The mental energy you expend when you forego doing it now – or judging yourself for not – is often far greater than the act of performing the task on deck. Tomorrow, cross another item off the list. In life, there will always be that eternal list of things to do. Addressing tasks – both big and small – can be cause for celebration at the end of each day. Whether you go at the pace of a snail or a cheetah, you'll be moving forward.

It's the job that's never started that takes longest to finish.

J. R. Tolkien

235

Activity Inspires Motivation

There will be times in life when a situation, person, or event leaves you inspired and propels you into action or a new way of being – having change occur effortlessly. Chances are, however, that you will experience more periods when you struggle to find momentum. It pays to develop an action–based philosophy. You're much more likely to become enthusiastic when you're moving towards something. Activity inspires motivation. When you initiate a course of action merely by getting started, you multiply the probability of restoring momentum. Action also interrupts dead end thought processes. Instead of waiting for the perfect job, take any job for the time being. Volunteer, to keep your mind occupied. Action dissipates worry so implement success structures that keep you active. Initiate one or two critical actions steps (CAS) that promise results. You can even trick yourself to staying on track. Prepay for your Personal Training sessions or Life Coach. Commit to presenting your Business Plan 30 days out to a group you know and trust. Little things like this can make a significant difference *if, how,* and *when* you make things happen.

The great aim of education is not knowledge but action.

Herbert Spencer

Chained to Email

Email has become a quick, efficient way to communicate, and it has also become a great waste of time. Imagine going to your snail mail box and checking it every 20 minutes? Chances are you wouldn't – it makes no sense. So STOP doing this with email. Turn off the auto-notification button on your computer – much like a ringing phone is not urgent, neither is most email. Checking email 5–20 times per day (which is about average) can consume hours. People who value their time learn to eliminate this behavior. Resolve to check email once or twice a day – if you must – and have an auto message stating that you will check messages twice a day (if necessary). This is a perfect way to free up time. Remember, being active is not necessarily time well spent.

Time is what we want most, but what we use worst.

William Penn

Anywhere Yoga

So you're in line at the bank, the grocery store, or waiting for a plane – whether you have 5 or 60 minutes, you could use the time as an opportunity to do a bit of subtle stretching. There are many exercises you can do to burn calories and stretch muscles, freeing up energy flow in the body while utilizing a few moments. Really, doing tiptoe extension takes mere moments, and over a month can make a difference in how your calves appear, not to mention burning off a few additional calories. Why not do a couple of lunges while waiting for the photocopy machine at work? Try subtly stretching your neck or the areas where tension gathers in your body. Loosen up those tight back muscles while waiting for your morning Java, or do butt clenches in the elevator. Seriously, doing so puts you in the moment immediately, instead of waiting for the future to happen. This is a great way to curtail mounting frustrations. It also connects you back to your body, which for many of us is an area of significant disconnect. By the end of the day you may have burned calories equivalent to a glass of wine. How fantastic! Now imagine the difference a year could make.

Yoga has a sly, clever way of short-circuiting the mental patterns that cause anxiety.

Baxter Bell

Zen Wisdom

Walk as if you are kissing the Earth with your feet.

Thich Nhat Hanh

Everyone Has Something to Teach

Wayne Dyer told this story when I saw him speak:

"A few years ago, at the Seattle Special Olympics, nine contestants, all physically or mentally disabled, assembled at the starting line for the 100-yard dash. At the sound of the gun, they all started out, not exactly in a dash, but with a relish to run the race to the finish and win. All, that is, except one little boy, who stumbled on the asphalt, tumbled over a couple of times, and began to cry. The other eight heard the boy cry. One at a time, they slowed down and looked back. Eventually they all turned around...every one of them. One girl with Down Syndrome bent down and kissed him and said, "This will make it better." Then all nine linked arms and walked together to the finish line. There was a standing ovation in the stadium and the cheering went on for several minutes."

Wayne then said, "And we have the nerve to call them mentally challenged."

Good leadership consists of showing average people
how to do the work of superior people.

John D. Rockefeller

Fertile Ground

If I were to consider my life as a piece of art or a painting, there have been days when I view the canvas and think it looks a lot like mud – little to be proud of – not realizing that Monet would paint soil and dirt before the delicate wildflowers could be added to his masterpiece. What appeared to be a muddy mess was in fact the perfect foundation for beauty to come.

Flowers grow out of darkness.

Corita Kent

Meet Others in Their World

Anne and Carol have been best friends for several years. Anne by all accounts is a hugger – someone who derives enjoyment from hugs. Though she loves people, Carol is not comfortable with hugs, and prefers that friends and family not expect this from her with any frequency. Though Anne has an urge to hug Carol as part of a greeting ritual, her awareness of the discomfort it causes for her friend takes precedence over her urge to express love her way. Funny thing is, every once in a while Carol initiates a hug with Anne, because she knows what it means to her. It's pretty easy to learn what works for others by being observant and simply following the lead that other people automatically provide you with. When you learn what works for others, not only is it gracious to follow suit by honoring their world, but it encourages harmony and ease.

The giving of love is an education in itself.

Eleanor Roosevelt

Verbal Reticence

The internal conversation of a human being is filled with fleeting thoughts, opinions, and observations. Your busy brain is being flooded at every second as it works to interpret information and situations. Many of these impulses are not share worthy, so be selective and choose wisely what you share with other people. Some people talk simply to make noise, showing little regard for what's being said, how it's landing or if it offers value. A gracious communicator will act consciously, use language that resonates, and most importantly, share information that piques the interest of the listener.

Take advantage of every opportunity to practice your communication skills so that when important occasions arise, you will have the gift, the style, the sharpness, the clarity, and the emotions to affect other people.

Jim Rohn

The Now

Consider that when you woke up this morning, expecting tomorrow, it was today again. I suspect the same will happen tomorrow, as it did yesterday. Suffice to say there is no tomorrow, no yesterday – only today, only this moment, The Now. Honor whatever it brings.

Breathe. Let go. And remind yourself that this VERY moment is the only one you know you have for sure.

Oprah Winfrey

Recognize the Signs

There was a man who was drowning. A boat came along, and the man on the boat asked, "Do you need help?" The man said, "God will save me." Then another boat came and tried to help him, but again the drowning man insisted, "God will save me." Eventually he succumbed to his exhaustions and drowned. When he arrived in heaven, the man spoke with God and said, "God, why didn't you save me?" God said, "I sent you two boats, you dummy!"

From the movie: The Pursuit of Happyness

Beware of false knowledge; it is more dangerous than ignorance.

George Bernard Shaw

Health & Happiness Traits

Much like having a healthy body, happiness is a series of daily choices. Working out a few times and eating a couple of healthy meals will not create an optimal physical state when done sporadically, but when practiced habitually, results are guaranteed. Health and happiness follow the same principles. It's through the regular direction of your attention to that which you are grateful for, and frequently letting go – or seeing beyond obstacles – that your happiness traits become engrained. This includes embracing strengths as opposed to becoming distracted by weaknesses. Make it a daily ritual to acknowledge what IS working in your life. Play the game of finding excuses to be happy. Like anything, the sooner you begin, the faster you'll start to see the benefits.

Our attitude toward life determines life's attitude towards us.

Earl Nightengale

Ask Questions

It was Thanksgiving and Elsa was lovingly preparing dinner for her family in her traditional country kitchen. Her adorable granddaughter Emily innocently inquired into one of her cooking practices. "Grandma, why is it you and Mommy always cut the ends off the ham?" "Come to think of it, I don't know my dear. My mother always did it this way." Elsa, inspired to answer her granddaughter's question, then called her mother overseas and asked. "Mom, I have been doing this for years without question, and your great-granddaughter just asked about it – so why is it you always cut the ends off when cooking a ham?" "My darling, I had only one pan – in order to make it fit I cut the ends off."

Author Unknown

The power to question is the basis of all human progress.

Indira Gandhi

Ignore the Naysayers

You have a dream, a beautiful vision of what's possible – but the people in your environment fail to see it as clearly as you do. In fact, some of them think you're crazy! Relinquish the urge to waste precious energy in an attempt to sway the opinion of the skeptics. You don't need to win them over – it's a gross misdirection of your life force. People that operate as though they know what's best for your life – or what's possible in general – simply don't have the courage to believe or pursue their own ideas. It's not that you can't – it's that they can't. Arguing with this type of personality feeds their plight and causes you to doubt yourself, so let them be. They are hardwired differently than you are. Nod and smile, and carry on with your irrational optimism (wink, wink) – because one day in the future, the opportunity may present itself where you can say, "I told you so." You probably won't say it because you have too much class, but the option will be presented all the same.

People who say it cannot be done should not interrupt those who are doing it.

George Bernard Shaw

The Wisdom of Generosity

A wise woman who was traveling in the mountains found a precious stone in a stream. The next day she met a traveler who was hungry, and the wise woman opened her bag to share her food. The hungry traveler saw the precious stone and asked the woman to give it to him. She did so without hesitation. The traveler left, rejoicing in his good fortune. He knew the stone was worth enough to give him security for a lifetime. But a few days later he came back to return the stone to the wise woman. "I've been thinking," he said. "I know how valuable the stone is, but I give it back in the hope that you can give me something even more precious. Give me what you have within you that enabled you to give me the stone."

Author Unknown

Real generosity is doing something nice for someone who will never find out.

Frank A. Clark

Operate from Workability

Bring your awareness to how often you label something good, bad, right, or wrong. When you tell yourself and others an action is wrong or bad, it implies judgment, which activates unproductive emotions that can result in feelings of guilt and inadequacy. Rarely does this aid in correcting the behavior – in fact, it's likely to perpetuate it. When you operate from the context of workability, it can offer power in relation to your own performance and the actions of others too. For example, it works when my boss expresses enthusiasm and acknowledges my contribution. It doesn't work when my teenage daughter comes home past her curfew. Or you may notice that reinforcing healthy food patterns works with your health goals. In reality, there is no right or wrong, good or bad – simply choice, opinion, and preference. Got it? So the next time you have the urge to label something right or wrong, call it from a workability perspective.

A different language is a different vision of life.

Federico Fellini

Zen Wisdom

In a tiny Mexican village, an American tourist complimented a local fisherman on the quality of his fish and asked how long it took him to catch them. "Not long," answered the Mexican. "So why didn't you stay out longer and catch more?" The Mexican explained that his small catch was sufficient to meet his needs. The tourist asked, "What about the rest of your time?" "I sleep late, play with my kids, and take a siesta with my wife. At night, I go into the village to see my friends. I play the guitar, sing a few songs...I have a very full life." The American interrupted, "I have an MBA from Harvard, and I can help you. Start by fishing longer every day, and sell the extra fish you catch. With the money, you can buy a bigger boat. Eventually you can buy several boats, until you have an entire fleet. You can also negotiate directly and maybe even open your own plant. You can then leave this little village and move to Mexico City, LA or even New York! From there you can direct your huge new enterprise." "How long would that take?" asked the Mexican. "Perhaps 25 years," the man replied. "And then?" replied the fisherman. "Well my friend, that's when it gets really interesting. When your business gets really big, you can start selling stocks and make millions!"

"Millions? Really? And then?" said the Mexican. "After that, you'll be able to retire, move to a little village near the coast, sleep late, play with your children, take a siesta with your wife, and spend your evenings playing the guitar and singing songs with your friends."

Author Unknown

The key to wisdom is knowing all the right questions.

John Simone